ESTHONIA

RUJIENA

VALKA

GAUJA R.

VALMIERA

SMILTENE

APE

ALUKSNE

Abrenes

VILAKA

jons

CESIS

SIGULDA

Gauje

JAUNPIE

rajo

ERGLI

MADONA

KARSAVA

PLAVINAS

VARAKLANI

VILANI

LUDZA

KRUSTPILS

REZEKNE

UNJELGAVA

JEKABPILS

LIVANI

ZILUPE

MALTA

NERETA

PREILI

DAGDA

AKNISTE

ILUKSTE

DAUGAVPILS

KRASLAVA

GRIVA

U.S.S.R.

POLAND

JOURNEY INTO TERROR

Story of the Riga Ghetto

JOURNEY INTO TERROR

Story of the Riga Ghetto

Gertrude Schneider

LTD
ARK HOUSE

NEW YORK

Ark House Ltd.
100 East 42nd Street
New York, New York 10017

Library of Congress Catalog Card No.: 79-57186
ISBN 0-935764-00-3

Printed in the United States of America

Contents

Preface

From the outside, it looked like any of the other ghettos in the East—complete with the ubiquitous barbed wire and the heavily armed guards. It was only when one was inside that the difference became apparent, for here, in the middle of Riga, the capital of Latvia, was a tiny German hamlet, scrupulously clean, complete with German street names, German police, German street cleaners, even German schools, and occasional strains of German music. One could hear the impeccable speech of people from Hanover, the flat twang of Berliners, the broad dialect of people from Leipzig and Dresden, the soft, lilting speech of Bavarians and Viennese, and the hard, but correct German spoken by Czechs. All those proper, middle-class people had one thing in common: They were Jews who had been deported to the east for liquidation but had been spared temporarily because their labor was needed. Here then, separated from its Latvian-Jewish counterpart, was the German-Jewish Ghetto of Riga.

Between November 27, 1941 and February 10, 1942, twenty transports amounting to a total of some 20,000 Jewish men, women, and children from Germany proper, from Austria, and from Czechoslovakia were deported to the Latvian capital, where they were herded into the ghetto. My parents, my younger sister, and I were part of the very last transport to reach Riga. Nothing in our former life in Vienna had prepared us for what lay ahead. Like those who came with earlier transports, we had no inkling of the true purpose for which we had been sent to the eastern territories recently conquered from Russia. We could not have imagined that the

term "resettlement," given in the official orders as the reason
for our deportation from Austria, was only a euphemism for
extermination. It was difficult to believe that we had been
marked for death, for on our arrival in the ghetto we found
ourselves surrounded by a society which in many ways was
supportive rather than destructive. Harsh though conditions
were, we thought we would be able to survive. Terror was an
occasional reminder of our precarious situation, but there
was always the hope of deliverance.

My father believed in keeping records. Accordingly, shortly before we left for the east, he gave me a diary and admonished me to write down all that I thought was important.
Neither he nor I imagined that his gift would eventually contain the seeds of a book about the Riga Ghetto. If there is
any purpose in the survival of one who has been burned, then
it must be so that he may tell about the fire. Using my diary
as one small source, I began a systematic research of the Riga
Ghetto, research that would occupy untold hours of exam-
ining documents and depositions, of interviewing scores of
survivors, and of subsequently evaluating the material. After
reading the literature available in the United States, mainly at
YIVO, the Jewish Institute for Scientific Research, I went
back to Riga, where I was greatly aided by the local Ministry
of Culture in gathering still more material. Occasionally, I
walked through what once had been the ghetto. Strangers
were living there, but I could almost feel the spirits of those
who had walked long ago on the same cobblestones, and who
had perished so senselessly. Thus reinforced in my desire to
write about the lives of these martyrs, I did much of my
subsequent research in Germany, Austria, and Czechoslovakia
with an even greater sense of urgency.

As a trained historian and despite my personal involvement, I believe that I owe my readers objectivity. I have tried
to remain detached, but it has not always been easy. After
all, the ghetto was the scene of my adolescence, of that mys-

terious interlude when one does not yet know one's destiny and is eager to turn into an adult in order to find out. It is only later on that one looks back with wonder and with great nostalgia. For most of my immediate friends there was never to be a later time. Their ashes have been scattered and, except for a handful of survivors, there is no one left to mourn. It is imperative that the dead be remembered, and I hope that my book will serve to keep their memory alive, long after all of us have turned to dust.

I acknowledge with gratitude the various individuals and institutions that aided me in my research. I am forever indebted to my mentor at the City University of New York, Professor Howard Adelson, whose help was invaluable, and to Professors Keith Eubank and Hans Trefousse, who gave unstintingly of their time. I am also grateful to the Ministry of Culture in Riga, to the Institut fuer Zeitgeschichte in Munich, to the International Tracing Service in Arolsen, Germany, and to the Juedische Gemeinden in Vienna, Berlin, and others. Special thanks go to the survivors of the Riga Ghetto who spent endless hours with me, recalling the past. Though their memories must have been painful to them at times, they never refused to be interviewed. My appreciation also goes to Dr. Barbara Bernheim, the editor of Ark House Ltd., who critically reviewed the final draft of this manuscript.

I could never have accomplished the research and writing without the patience and understanding of my husband Eric. I also want to thank my children, David, Barbara, and Peter, for having been tolerant of the many haphazard meals and the frequent absences of their mother in the course of her work on this book.

My father did not live to see the dawn of freedom. I therefore dedicate this book to his memory and to his insistence that accurate records be kept.

Gertrude Schneider

JOURNEY INTO TERROR

Story of the Riga Ghetto

Introduction

Much has been written about the wrenching experience of the Nazi Holocaust. To be sure, all that literature was meant to be read and understood by the world at large. Actually, it has reached only a limited audience, primarily Jews and a few historians, sociologists, and psychologists looking for source material.

Not so the Riga Ghetto. While it constitutes a very small segment of the immense subject of the Holocaust, it served as the backdrop for a best-selling novel, *The Odessa File* by Frederick Forsythe, that was later made into a film.[1] The Riga Ghetto was also the subject of four memoirs, three of them published. It is also mentioned in a number of postwar German novels as well as in the book *Wanted!* by Howard Blum, which treats the story of Nazis in the United States; the Riga Ghetto, albeit erroneously, serves as the basis for one of the chapters.[2]

Although it is claimed that *The Odessa File* is based on fact, it is clearly fictitious and contains many statements to which former inmates of the ghetto have good cause to take exception. For instance, Mr. Forsythe gives the impression that only those individuals who fulfilled official functions in the ghetto administration were able to survive. Nothing could be further from the truth. Among the survivors, for instance, of whom slightly over six hundred are alive today, only a few held official positions in the ghetto.

Of the three published memoirs, one, *Die Vernichtung der Juden Lettlands* by Max Kaufmann, concerns the Latvian Jews and their destruction.[3] The other two, *Sadismus oder*

Wahnsinn? by Jeanette Wolff and *One Who Came Back* by Josef Katz, deal with the experience of the Jewish deportees from Germany in the Riga Ghetto.[4] The fourth memoir, unpublished to date, was written by Gerda Gottschalk, a young Catholic woman who shared the experience of the Jews because her parents had been Jewish at birth and thus, under Nazi "racial" law, so was she. Her account is concerned with the "German" ghetto,* but it differs in scope from that of Jeannette Wolff chiefly because of the difference in age between the two women.

All of these accounts were written immediately after World War II, when the gruesome events were still vivid in the minds of the writers. In the three published accounts especially, it seems that the enormity of the personal sufferings of the authors left no place for an objective description of life in the ghetto as it really was, a life which existed and went on parallel to the horrible events that in the end were to engulf everything and everyone in their path.

Yet it is only an objective report of daily life which can show that this particular ghetto was unique, but at the same time a microcosm and a mirror of the larger world outside. Only a brief section of Katz's book is concerned with the ghetto, he was there but a short time; yet he is aware of the cultural activities which were carried on there. Miss Gottschalk, too, writes about daily life in the ghetto; perhaps because of her youth or her unbroken faith in God, she saw a different aspect from those perceived by Max Kaufmann and Jeanette Wolff who were then already middle aged.

---

*The terms "German ghetto" and "Latvian ghetto" used throughout this book refer to the two sectors into which the Riga Ghetto was divided, one for the Jewish deportees from Germany, Austria, and Czechoslovakia, and the other for Latvian Jews and Jews who were living in Latvia at the time that the country was overrun by the German armies.

Kaufmann was mourning his wife and son. He believed that the Latvian Jews had been exterminated to make room for the Jewish deportees from Germany, for when he wrote his book, the sources proving otherwise were not available as yet. His dejection is therefore understandable. He devotes hardly any attention to daily existence in either the German or the Latvian ghettos of Riga. The book reads like an unending tale of atrocity after atrocity, of murder after murder, with fear and hunger as constant companions. To be sure, these horrors were always present. But so were love and hope, a firm determination to make the best of things, and so were kindness and a belief in a better future.

Like Kaufmann, Jeanette Wolff, who had been politically active in her native Saxony and who became a member of the German Bundestag (House of Deputies) after World War II, enumerates the horrors faced by the deportees and describes the continuous slaughter. She, too, fails to depict the living and breathing community within the ghetto and the efforts that were expended on preserving some kind of cultural life and thus the sanity of the inmates. As is often the case with personal memoirs, Mrs. Wolff is not always accurate as far as dates and figures are concerned. At the end of her book, she extends her hand to the Germans in an effort to "build bridges."

Kaufmann's book as well as that of Jeanette Wolff, errors and all, were used as sources by Raul Hilberg in *The Destruction of European Jews* and by Gerald Reitlinger in *The Final Solution.*[5] Depositions made by survivors were also used, although it was hard for these witnesses, having been actual inmates of the ghetto, to develop an overall perspective of the whole story. All that they could see was themselves and their immediate world, the rest was mostly conjecture. Judging the number of victims was difficult, and dates were easily forgotten. Of course, not knowing the entire story might have been beneficial, for in an experience such as this, where loss of hope meant certain death, ignorance was indeed bliss.

To avoid errors, depositions had to be compared with official German records, individual recollections had to be matched against others, and extreme care had to be exercised to avoid the usual clichés. The story of the Riga Ghetto is therefore not merely another report of mass killings and atrocities. Of necessity, those crimes will be mentioned, but only in passing. The scope of my story is the creation, and the eventual destruction of an old fashioned—almost medieval—ghetto of Jews from central Europe that was attached to an older ghetto of Lavian Jews but was autonomous and thus separate from the latter. It is the story of Jews who found themselves not only deprived of their freedom but deported to an alien land, Jews who thought that they would be able to buy time by being compliant. It is the story of the people of Riga's "German" ghetto who attempted to cling to a distinctly cultural life at a time when millions of their brothers and sisters were being put to death, hoping that by giving their lives a semblance of normalcy, they would be able to avoid the destiny that was planned for them by Adolf Hitler. On January 30, 1939, Hitler declared in an address to the Reichstag (the German parliament) that "if war comes, brought about by international financiers, the result will be the destruction of the Jewish race in Europe."[6] Because the war against Poland and subsequently against Russia brought additional millions of Jews into the German Reich, his words were to assume frightening accuracy.

In the larger cities of Poland whole neighborhoods were set aside for the creation of ghettos that were to contain Jews from those cities as well as from the surrounding countryside. Deportees from the Reich were then added to those crowded communities, aggravating conditions that already made life practically unbearable.

Ghettos were set up also in the territories conquered from

Russia; they were usually in the worst sections of the cities, not too far from the forests that later served as ideal sites for wholesale murder. To this end, the ghetto of Minsk employed the forest at Mogilev Road, the ghetto of Lwow the Janowska Road, and the ghetto of Kovno the old Russian forts; the ghetto of Vilno the pits at Ponary, and the ghetto of Riga first, the Rumbula Forest and later, the Bikerniek Forest nearby. Jewish deportees arriving from the Reich were often brought straight to these sites of slaughter. In Minsk, the first contingents of deportees were incorporated into the ghetto, but most of them were liquidated within a few months.

Life in these ghettos was even worse than in the ghettos of Poland. Apart from physical discomfort, there was the realization that essentially the ghettos were only temporary communities. From the time of the German invasion to the establishment of the ghettos, the native Jews had experienced enough brutal treatment to make it clear to them that their days were numbered. A series of German victories on the eastern front and the apathy of the world to the fate of the Jews encouraged the German government to proceed with that systematic liquidation of the Jews referred to in Nazi parlance as the "Final Solution of the Jewish Problem."

1
The Jews of Riga

In 1939, when the Baltic lands became part of the Russian sphere of influence, the Jews of Latvia, then numbering about 93,000, found themselves in a dilemma. After the outright annexation of Latvia by the Soviet Union in 1940, this dilemma became even more complex, for there were some Jews who greeted the communists with open arms. The Latvian communists, of course, shared this joy, but the majority of the Latvian population hated the Soviet invaders almost as much as they hated the Jews and became even more ferocious in their anti-Semitism.[7] The Soviet authorities were well aware of their hatred and in an effort to stem the tide, both Jewish and non-Jewish communists held meetings at which anti-Semitism was condemned as a device to divert attention from the true class struggle against capitalism.

The majority of Latvians never noticed that in fact, the Russians were persecuting the large Jewish middle class, nor did they take note of the treatment accorded to the small number of Jews who had come to then independent Latvia from Germany, Austria, and Czechoslovakia in 1938 and 1939, not as deportees but as "illegal" immigrants seeking a place of refuge from Nazi oppression. Instead of helping those unfortunate people, the Soviet authorities assigned them to forced labor, to build roads and public works projects.

The fact that they belonged to the hated bourgeoisie was to save some of the Latvian Jews, because the Soviets deported them to eastern Siberia and Soviet Mongolia only a week before the German invasion.

The Nazis attacked the Soviet Union on June 22, 1941. Some time before, Reinhard Heydrich, the chief of the *Sicherheitspolizei* (Security Police) and the *Sicherheitsdienst* (Security Service, commonly called S.D.)* created four *Einsatzgruppen* (special task forces) A, B, C, and D that were to serve in the occupied territories. *Einsatzgruppe A*, led by Dr. Franz Stahlecker who held the SS rank of *Brigade-fuehrer*,** would be responsible for the imposition of the "Final Solution" in Latvia, a country that was to become one great charnel house.

On July 1, 1941, the Germans marched into Riga, the capital of Latvia and the final chapter of Riga's Jewish community, numbering 40,000 men, women, and children, began. Many Latvians helped the German invaders by committing unbelievable atrocities against the Jews and even joined the SS in order to be part of the Nazi hierarchy.

On July 7, less than a week after their arrival in the city, *Einsatzgruppe A* organized a pogrom in Riga and reported that 400 Jews had been killed. As evidenced by photographs, the actual slaying had been done by Latvians and not Germans. The Nazis described this outrage as a "self-cleansing" operation. In his report to SS Chief Heinrich Himmler, Dr. Stahlecker, the head of the group, stated that no other operations of that nature had taken place in his domain.

Stahlecker must have been referring to operations organized by the Germans. They did not have to make an extra effort, considering the conditions that normally prevailed at Riga's Central Prison, a site of the most brutal murders, or at the Riga Police Prefecture, which was presided over by Roberts Stiglics. Stahlecker might have overlooked the

---

*Nazi party intelligence service created by SS Chief Heinrich Himmler.
**SS rank equivalent to major general in the regular army.

Perkonkrusts, the Latvian fascists, who, under the able leadership of *Strumbannfuehrer** Victors Arajs, a Latvian, murdered at least 2,000 Jews during July and August 1941 alone. The *Perkonkrusts* concentrated on the well-to-do, in order to be able to confiscate their property. In the Great Synagogue of Riga, a gang led by that same Victors Arajs, Herbert Cukurs, and Vilis Hazners, incinerated alive several hundred Jews, chiefly women and children.[8]

The Riga press did its best to fan the hatred of the Latvian populace for the Jews. Articles appeared such as that printed on July 11, 1941, most fittingly titled "The Jew—Source of Our Destruction." The article ended with a statement that because the Jews had sought to destroy the Latvian nation, they could not be permitted to survive as a national or a cultural entity and therefore, all the Jews would have to die.[9]

By October 25, 1941, all Jews living in Riga had been brought into the ghetto, which was located in a section called Moscow Suburb. This process had taken so long simply because the Gentiles who had lived in that area had to be forced to leave before the Jews could move in. It is hard to understand why these Gentiles should have put up so much resistance; the houses were old, dilapidated, and badly in need of repair. Eventually about 33,000 Jews were contained in a space large enough for perhaps only one-third of that number. The threat of epidemics was great.[10]

Notwithstanding the inhuman conditions under which they were forced to live, the Jews in the ghetto worked regularly, because their services were commandeered by the enormous Nazi war machine and because they depended on whatever they earned, having been deprived of their former livelihoods. They made the best of circumstances. A "Jewish Committee" was created along with a Jewish police force to

---

*SS rank equivalent to major in the regular army.

keep order inside the ghetto. There was a labor committee that assigned jobs according to demands made by German authorities. The ghetto even boasted of a small hospital, the *Linas Hazedek,* and there were, of course, numerous doctors, including the noted Dr. Vladimir Mintz who had once operated on Lenin. While there were enough doctors, there were very few drugs and medicines, and there was much trepidation about the coming winter. Yet the Jews need not have worried, for they had only thirty-five days left to live.

On November 27, 1941, the inmates of the ghetto were notified that they would be moved out of the ghetto and "resettled" elsewhere. On November 28, specific streets had to be evacuated, and the Jews were told to gather in front of their houses on the next day. That evening, the Latvian SS led by Herbert Cukurs, and the German SS, led by *Sturmbannfuehrer* Rudolf Lange, head of a group referred to as *Einsatzkommando* (special detail) 2 C, swarmed through the streets hunting for Jews. Children were thrown from windows, women were pushed down flights of stairs, shots were fired, and people fell, wounded or dead.

Half dead from terror, the survivors lined up in long columns. Over 15,000, heavily guarded by both Latvian and German SS, were marched toward the Rumbula Forest. The very old, the sick, and very young children made the trip in buses. In the forest, graves had been prepared for them by Soviet prisoners of war, but some of the victims had to spend days awaiting their turn. They were forced to stand outdoors in the bitter cold, watching the massacre, knowing that they would be next. They probably either waited for a miracle or else they prayed that the end might come soon. Although they were under close and constant guard, one of the victims managed to write a little note that was later found and brought back into the ghetto. It said simply, "Don't forget us—take revenge." This note prompted Max Kaufmann after the war to tell the story of the destruction of Latvian Jewry.

Meanwhile, those Jews remaining behind had cleared the streets and apartments of corpses, and had buried them in the ghetto cemetery. The next day they went back to work as usual.

As has already been stated, the organization responsible for the liquidation of Jews in Latvia was *Einsatzgruppe A.* Each of the four Einsatzgruppen had so-called Einsatzkommandos and *Sonderkommandos* (special details) that took care of the actual executions. They were supported by the *Sicherheitsdienst,* commonly called the S.D., the Nazi party intelligence service.

Einsatzkommando 2C, which was part of Einsatzgruppe A in Riga, was headed by *Sturmbannfuehrer* Dr. Rudolf Lange. Reitlinger referred to him as "Fritz" Lange possibly because he signed all documents "Dr. Lange," without writing his first name. Hilberg called him "Otto" Lange, probably for the same reason. In a booklet published by the Director of Prosecutions in Herford, Germany, in 1946, he is listed as "Hans" Lange. According to that document, he was being held prisoner in the British zone, but as late as 1972, the West German authorities in Hamburg, who handled all Nazi war-crime cases pertaining to the Baltic states, declared that the former commander of the S.D. in the city of Riga, "Dr. jus, Rudolf Lange," born in 1910, had committed suicide in the fortress of Posen in 1945 so as not to be taken alive by the Red Army. According to one statement in *NS Prozesse,* however, the Soviets did take him prisoner, and his fate is unknown. His wife or widow Elsa, who now lives in Mannheim, may be the only person who knows the truth.

Lange usually supervised the executions, and the Latvian SS troops helped with the grim task. These troops were attached to the *Sonderkommando* and performed the actual task of shooting the victims at the edge of the enormous mass graves so that the bodies would fall right into them. Thus, while the Germans provided the expert guidance, the

Latvians only too willingly did the "dirty" work. At his trial after the war, *Obergruppenfuehrer* * Friedrich Jeckeln, the *Hoehere SS und Polizeifuehrer Gruppe Nord,* who was attached to all the *Einsatzgruppen* with his mobile killing units, credited the Latvians with "strong nerves for executions of this sort."

The carnage was repeated in almost the same manner on December 8, 1941. The last Jews to be exterminated left the ghetto in the morning hours of December 9. Thus, one of the oldest, most distinguished Jewish communities of eastern Europe was virtually wiped out.

There are discrepancies in the number of Jews killed during those ten bloody days. Reitlinger, who preferred to underestimate, stated that at least 24,000 were murdered, but Dr. Stahlecker, the leader of the *Einsatzgruppe* actually involved, estimated the number at 27,000, which is closer to the figure arrived at by Max Kaufmann, who said that the number must have been in excess of 27,000. Kaufmann included the Jews—probably overlooked by Stahlecker in his report—who had not been taken into the forest but had already been murdered inside the ghetto. Stahlecker, however, added to the number of victims a contingent of German Jews deported from the Reich, who had left Berlin on November 27, 1941. Therefore the actual number of victims must have been still higher; most likely, it was 29,000.

If the arrival of this particular transport, from Berlin, which carried 1,000 Jews, followed the usual pattern of later arrivals, it was received at Skirotava Station by the ubiquitous *Sturmbannfuehrer* Rudolf Lange who then escorted its occupants to the forest, an accomplishment which he then described, in great detail, at the Wannsee Conference. This

---

*SS rank equivalent to general in the regular army.

conference in Berlin, at which only 14 persons, all high Nazi officials, participated, had been called by the indefatigable Reinhard Heydrich to give more explicit guidelines on the implementation of the "Final Solution" in the eastern territories.

According to Kaufmann, about 5,000 Latvian Jews were left in Riga after December 9. Most were males who held jobs vital to the war effort. With the exception of 300 young women, all Jewish females as well as all children of both sexes had been killed. Stahlecker, in his graphic report to Himmler, listed only 2,500 on hand in the Riga Ghetto. He evidently did not include those Jews who were not sent back to the ghetto at the end of each working day, but were kept at their places of employment in an effort to conserve precious time and manpower.

The 300 women were taken to the Central Prison just before the last *Aktion,* or "operation," of December 8, 1941. One Latvian SS man who has remained nameless, urged several of them to go to the prison "for their own good." When the women were brought back into the ghetto after the massacre, they were put into one house, separated from the men and also from the area that would become known as the "German" ghetto, where the Jews arriving from Germany, Austria, and Czechoslovakia, were to live in strict separation from the Latvian Jews. As these women whose lives had been spared were led back into the ghetto, the men who had survived the massacre in the ghetto itself, watched in silence by the barbed-wire fences. The women kept their eyes lowered so as not to have to see the agony in the faces of the men who had lost their wives and children.[11] Once again, the people who were slain inside the ghetto were buried by those who had remained alive.

The aftermath of this carnage was a furious exchange of letters between the German Army and the SS. There were complaints about how this "operation" had cut into the badly needed labor force. The army did not know where to find replacements since the local Gentile population was neither trained nor sufficient in number to take the place of the slain Jews. While these complaints were of no avail to those Jews who had already been put to death, they helped prolong the lives of the Jewish deportees from the Reich who had begun to arrive in Riga in November, 1941.

Logistics decreed that these new arrivals should be gathered in one place since this would make it easier for the authorities to make "selections"* and perform executions. They therefore decided to build one large concentration camp in the village of Salaspils for these Jews, about an hour's distance from Riga. While Camp Salaspils was being built, the Jews were brought to Jumpramuize, later renamed Jungfernhof. They were to stay in both Salaspils and Jungfernhof for only as long as it would take to eliminate the majority of the inmates. The Moscow Suburb of Riga proper, the site of the original ghetto, had not figured in the initial plans of Dr. Lange, but seeing that Salaspils and Jungfernhof were more than an hour away from the city and from the war plants and army bases where the Jews were to work, he foresaw the need for quartering later transports in the original ghetto, in the houses left vacant by the Latvian Jews who had been killed. In this way a separate ghetto was created for the Jewish deportees from Germany, Austria, and Czechoslovakia, to become known as the "German" ghetto. Jungfernhof eventually became a slave labor farm; Salaspils became a labor camp for males only, as well as a transit camp for Jews on their way to the forest—and to death.

---

*In "selections" the inmates would be lined up before the Nazi officials. Those classified as fit for work were ordered to move to one side, usually to the right. Those found unfit for work were told to move to the other side and were subsequently exterminated.

As late as November 1941, there were still some doubts in the Nazi minds about the projected plan of transferring Jews from the Reich to Riga; it was therefore decided that the first five trainloads be sent to Kovno, in central Lithuania, which had also been occupied by the Nazis. A letter dated December 4, 1941, even mentions Pleskau (Pskov), a city 100 miles further east, as an alternate destination for the deportees.

In regard to the question of sparing the lives of Jews whose skills were considered essential for the war effort, until November 1941, instructions from Berlin were explicit. No exception was to be made. As for the Jewish deportees arriving from the Reich, it was made equally clear that their stay in Salaspils and Jungfernhof would only be temporary. The telegram containing this message is dated November 9, 1941, and bears an ominous notation requesting the recipient to get in touch with Obergruppenfuehrer Friedrich Jeckeln, the officer in charge of the hard-working mobile killing units.

The massacre of the Latvian Jews followed in late November and early December, and the complaints pouring into Berlin resulted in a temporary reprieve for the new arrivals from Germany. To the uninitiated, however, the situation looked entirely different. By now, it has become quite clear that this impression was erroneous, but for a long time the Latvian Jews who had survived the slaughter believed that their own families had been murdered simply so that there would be room in the ghetto area to accommodate the Jewish deportees from the Reich who, through adherence to a diabolical master plan, would be kept alive. Neither the Latvian Jews nor their German companions in adversity could have known about the angry exchange of letters between the German Army and the SS about the loss of precious manpower caused by the murder of the Latvian Jews. As it was, given the traditional atmosphere of unfounded mistrust between German and Latvian Jews, the massacre became a wedge driving the two groups even further apart.

Neither group realized that the Jews who had arrived in Riga from Germany, Austria, and Czechoslovakia, had been marked for slaughter no less than the Jews who had been living in Latvia all along.

It is to the eternal credit of the surviving Latvian Jews that despite their feelings of resentment, they helped the newcomers from the Reich over the hurdles of the first shock of cold and hunger; it was they who smuggled milk into the ghetto for the children of the German Jews, children who, for the time being, were permitted to live and who must have been bitter reminders of those whose own children had been so brutally murdered only a few days before.

Unlike the newcomers from Germany, the Latvian Jews still had money with which to buy things. They also had valuables and, having lived in Riga all their lives, knew the city well. They were thus able to procure food much easier than the German Jews could ever have hoped to do.

Kaufmann wrote that the German Jews were strangers to the Latvian Jews and remained so until the end.[12] This statement might have been true in his own circle of middle-aged men, but it was certainly not true of the young people in the Latvian ghetto. To be sure, there were difficulties, aggravated by tactless people on both sides, but to a great extent, these problems were deliberately cultivated by the Nazi authorities.

On the positive side and despite the strict separation enforced by the Nazis between the two ghettos, the people of the Latvian and German ghettos did help each other in many ways, materially as well as emotionally. The Latvian ghetto was an all-male society—the majority of the women having been killed. Most of the men who had survived in the Latvian ghetto were young, healthy, and lonely for female companionship. The situation in the German ghetto was the reverse: most of the young men in the transports of deportees from the Reich had been taken to Camp Salaspils, leaving many girls and young women without men. An additional factor which often helped bring the two groups together was the comparative affluence of the Latvian Jews and the hunger that prevailed in the German ghetto. Love could be bought just as easily as it could be genuinely merited. Kaufmann, incidentally, stated that it was "unwise" of the young Latvian Jewish men to bring food to the Jewish women from Germany.[13]

In any event, the Jewish girls from Germany and the Jewish boys from Latvia cooperated to fill each other's physical and emotional needs, exactly as young people do in a world without barbed wires. In many cases, relationships were formed which continued for the duration of the ghetto as well as subsequently in Kaiserwald, a camp to which the inmates were transferred after the complete liquidation of the Riga Ghetto. Some of them have endured to this day.

2
Jews from the Reich

Plans for the deportation of Jews from the Reich to the Baltic states and of their extermination upon arrival had been made as early as October, 1941, when Dr. Alfred Wetzel, a member of the Ministry for Occupied Territories, wrote to *Reichskommissar* Hinrich Lohse that it would be much easier to build gas chambers in Riga than in the Reich proper and that Jews from Germany, Austria, and Czechoslovakia were scheduled to arrive in Riga shortly. At no time was there a suggestion that the German Jews should be brought to Riga as replacements for the native Jews slated for destruction; the German Jews, too, were to be exterminated, and they were shipped east for solely that reason. However, the erection of gas chambers proved unnecessary thanks to the work of *Einsatzgruppe A* and its auxiliaries. To facilitate matters, gas vans were often used for the extermination of children and old people. In this way, the others would not be slowed down on their march from the railroad station to the forest.

The German Jewish deportees came from villages, towns, and cities. Most of them were middle-class people, former shopkeepers, teachers, lawyers, and physicians, totally unprepared for the shock that awaited them. The onset of the persecution they had experienced had been gradual, and many of them could have left Germany sometime between 1933, when Hitler assumed power, and 1939, when the war broke out. But evidently they had felt so secure, so "German," that many of them considered the very idea of leaving their country unthinkable. By the time they realized that they should have left, it was too late.

There had been transports of Jewish deportees from Germany to Poland during 1940 and 1941; the cities of Minsk, Kovno, and Riga were next to serve as transit camps on the way to destruction.

With only those personal effects that they could carry, the Jews from the Reich were on their way once more. They had been told only that they were going to Riga. They were apprehensive, but none of them could imagine the brutal reality that they would have to confront. Those who were sent to the forest immediately at least did not suffer for long. Of those who reached the ghetto, some collapsed almost at once, but others, after the initial trauma, were able to delude themselves into believing that in spite of their desperate situation, they would eventually come out alive.

The men in charge of this phase of the Final Solution were *Brigadefuehrer* Dr. Franz Stahlecker and *Sturmbannfuehrer* Dr. Rudolf Lange. Both were aware of the fact that *Reichskommissar* Hinrich Lohse had objected to having Jews from the Reich come to Latvia. In order to placate Lohse, Lange sent Lohse a long letter, outlining what was to be done with the arriving Jews. He told him that he would need both Camps Salaspils and Jungfernhof for them, and he also wrote that if at all feasible, the first five transports originally intended for Riga should go to Kovno instead. In his next letter to Lohse, Lange wrote that transports of Jewish deportees had begun to arrive in Minsk, and that the first five transports originally destined for Riga were definitely going to Kovno. As late as December 4, 1941, the Minister for the Occupied Eastern Territories wrote to Lohse of a conversation that he had had with Reinhard Heydrich, in which the latter had told the Minister about the alternative site of Pleskau.

The massacre of the Latvian Jews on November 29 and December 8 deprived the German war plants and army installations of badly needed personnel. Both Salaspils and Jungfernhof were too far from the capital to furnish daily labor details. Accordingly, the plan was made to put the arrivals from the Reich into that now empty section of the Riga Ghetto. Because the various departments were not always aware of one another's plans, a letter dated December 18, 1941, to Lohse from the Minister for the Occupied Territories, mentioned that the needs of the war effort should not be considered in planning the fate of the Jews. In another letter, however, Hinrich Lohse himself asked the SS and police leaders in Reval, Riga, Kovno, and Minsk, to prevent the liquidation of skilled workers who were needed in military installations. Jewish though they were; and at the same time, he asked that a quick training program be inaugurated for the "natives."

As planned, the first five transports originally earmarked for Riga, went to Kovno instead. The first came from Munich, leaving that city on November 15, 1941; the second, from Berlin, leaving on November 17; the next one from Frankfurt, leaving on November 22, the fourth from Vienna, leaving on November 23, and the fifth, from Breslau, also leaving on November 23. The Gestapo lists are marked "no survivors" and they are correct, since the deportees were taken to Fort No. 9 in Kovno where the first three contingents were murdered on November 25, and the last two on November 29.[14]

The next transport, which left Berlin on November 27, was the one that Stahlecker had mentioned in his report to Himmler and to which Lange probably owed the honor of having been invited to the Wannsee Conference. All the deportees from Berlin, with the exception of a few young men, were added to the group of doomed Latvian Jews and joined them in their mass graves in the Rumbula Forest. The few young men who unloaded the luggage at Skirotava were sent to Camp Jungfernhof. They were joined there the next day by a contingent of Jews from Nuremberg, which also included Jews from Wuerzburg, Fuerth, and other neighboring small towns.

The commanding officer of Camp Jungernhof was *Oberscharfuehrer** Rudolf Seck who ordered the inmates to clean up the former troop barracks and set up a kitchen. He then appointed one of the men, a Mr. Kleeman, "camp elder." Conditions were appalling: People became sick, and many of them died. It was impossible to bury the dead because the ground was so frozen that it could not be dug. It was therefore decided that the corpses be stored in a shed. Eventually, by the end of January 1942, the commandant had the ground dynamited, so that the approximately 500 dead could be buried.[15]

In December, 1941, three more transports arrived at Camp Jungfernhof. They came from Stuttgart, Hamburg, and Vienna, bringing the population of the camp to almost 4,000. Whenever a transport from the Reich pulled in at the station of Skirotava, Dr. Lange, who in the meantime had been promoted to the rank of *Obersturmbannfuehrer,** was there with his sidekick, *Obersturmfuehrer*** Gerhard Maywald, to "greet" the victims. On the day that the Hamburg transport arrived, the weather was extremely cold. Because of this, one young fellow, Werner Koppel, was not able to open the door of the train fast enough. He paid for it with his life; Lange shot him on the spot.[16]

In retrospect, this rash act was unusual for Lange. He did most of his shooting only after the people had been brought into the camps. At the station he usually held himself in check, so as not to unduly alarm the arrivals. His nervousness that day might have been caused by the fact that at precisely the time of the arrival of the contingent from Hamburg, the

---

*SS rank equivalent to sergeant major in the regular army.

*SS rank equivalent to lieutenant colonel in the regular army.
**SS rank equivalent to first lieutenant in the regular army.

final phase of the slaughter of the Latvian Jews was taking place not too far away.

At Camp Jungfernhof, a few days later, a group of young men was selected by Seck and sent to Salaspils to build a new camp, supposedly for all the other Jews coming from the Reich. But this camp never became what it had been intended to be; instead, it remained an all-male camp until August, 1942. After that date, Russian prisoners of war and Latvian political prisoners were quartered there and put to work sorting some of the belongings taken from subsequent transports of Jews from the Reich, who passed through Salaspils on the way to their death in the forest (an exception was made for small children who were held back for a variety of experiments).[17]

In the forest adjoining the camp, graves had been prepared by the inmates. After they had undressed, the victims were either shot immediately at the edge of the graves or else they were ordered to lie face down between the legs of those already shot, and were then killed. The latter method saved much-needed space. It was invented by *Obergruppenfuehrer* Friedrich Jeckeln, who called it *"Sardinenpackung"* (sardine packaging). Ironically, this method could even save a victim's life, as in the case of Jeanette Wolff's son-in-law, who worked his way out of the grave after dark and somehow got back into the ghetto.

On December 10, 1941, a transport of Jews from Cologne was brought directly into the ghetto. The streets had not as yet been completely cleaned after the massacre of the Latvian Jews. The German Jews were horrified to see the evidence of the slaughter that was being cleared away by the Latvian Jews who had survived. The latter had been at work since the previous day, after having been ordered to clear the streets of all dead bodies. When they saw the Jews from Germany enter the ghetto, it seemed to them that they had been told to clean up the streets and houses to prepare proper accommodations for the new arrivals, and this, they felt, could have only one meaning: The Latvian Jews, their own people, had been killed to make room in the ghetto for the Jews from Germany.[18]

The Jews from Cologne, numbering about 1,000, were the first German Jews to enter the Riga Ghetto. As they straggled in, after having walked seven kilometers in the cold from the station, they were "welcomed" at the gate by *SS Obersturm-fuehrer* Kurt Krause who announced that he was the commandant of the ghetto. He immediately ordered one of the men, Manfred Leiser, to assume the leadership of the group. Leiser's official title was to be *Lageraeltester,* meaning literally "camp elder." Another deportee, Herbert Schultz, was appointed *Arbeitseinsatz,* which meant that he would be responsible for organizing *Kommandos* or labor details, to be sent to the city, where they would help in the German war effort. Commandant Krause left no doubt in the minds of his listeners that they had been brought from Germany to Riga simply to do war work. He also told them that their being German had been an important factor in their selection for these jobs; unlike the non-Germans, they would have no difficulty following instructions given in the German language.

The Latvian Jews who were cleaning the streets listened to Krause's speech with mounting resentment and despair, while the new arrivals from Germany, though horrified at the sight of blood and corpses still in the streets of the ghetto, felt secure in the belief that their being German did indeed make them more important than the Latvian Jews and therefore safe from harm.

The next day, December 11, 1941, *Generalkommissar* Drechsler, another official concerned with the "Jewish problem," wrote a sharp letter to *Obersturmbannfuehrer* Dr. Lange, chiding him for having brought these German Jews into the ghetto and asking him not to send any more. The main reason for Drechsler's displeasure with this "shipment" of new inmates was the fact that his people had not had sufficient time to remove the valuables left in the ghetto by the murdered Latvian Jews.

From Drechsler's letter it appears obvious that in arranging for the transport to be sent to the ghetto, Lange had not consulted the local German authorities but had evidently been following new orders received from Berlin. Lange continued to bring more Jews to the ghetto, but he cooperated with Drechsler to the extent of assigning only certain houses as living quarters to the Jews from Germany. They were strictly forbidden to enter other buildings. These were kept off limits until they had been thoroughly searched by Drechsler's subordinates, who looked mainly for jewelry, money, and furs, but left other things behind.

When the new arrivals entered the houses assigned to them, they found food, frozen solid, still on plates, dentures frozen in glasses of water wherever they had been left by the former occupants at the time of their hasty departure to their deaths. Often, the newcomers also discovered frozen corpses, which had been overlooked by the clean-up details and which they later had to bury themselves. It took them months to scrub off the many bloodstains they saw on the walls, the floors, and the steps of their new homes.

On the day following their arrival, columns of Jews from Germany joined their Latvian fellow Jews and marched out of the ghetto to clear the snow from the streets of the city. Only children and some mothers with infants, as well as a few men exempted by camp elder or ghetto elder Leiser and labor group organizer Schultz, remained in the ghetto. The men thus singled out were to form the German Jewish police force for the Cologne group. The Latvian Jews had their own ghetto police.

The German ghetto and the Latvian ghetto were separated by a barbed-wire fence, extending the entire length of Ludzas

Iela, the street which divided the two ghettos. Only when the inmates of the two ghettos met at work, outside, were they able to speak to each other; in that way the newcomers found out the gruesome details of what had befalled the former occupants of the houses to which they had been assigned.

Most of the German Jews, however, having been permitted to stay together as families, did not foresee a similar fate for themselves. Commandant Krause, and later other members of his staff, had told them that the ghetto had been prepared especially for them because, being able to speak German, they were "different" and much better qualified than their Latvian co-religionists to help in the war effort. Thus, once they had gotten over their initial shock from the sights of death and bloodshed, the inmates of the German ghetto felt that whatever had happened to the Latvian Jews could not possibly happen to them.

The unsuspecting newcomers could not have known that it had taken the Germans much serious reflection to decide not to kill the deportees from Germany immediately but to allow them to remain alive only as long as they proved to be useful workers. Once their strength had given out, they, too, would be killed. Nor could they have guessed that, contrary to Krause's protestations, the local German authorities were to record that the murdered Latvian Jews could have been much greater assets to the war effort because many of them had been craftsmen and skilled workers while most of the German Jews, who had been in business and in the professions before the war, could be used only for unskilled labor.

On December 12, 1941, a transport arrived from the west German city of Cassel, bringing Jews not only from Cassel but also from smaller towns such as Fulda and Eschwege. From that transport, Commandant Krause selected a man whom he dubbed *Gruppenaeltester,* or "group elder." He also put another man in charge of the organization of labor details for the group. It was further decreed that Leiser, as "ghetto elder," would be head of all the groups in the German ghetto, but that each group would have an elder of its own, who would be responsible to Leiser. Schultz was selected to head the labor detail administration for the entire German ghetto, with one person from each group reporting directly to him.

The talkative Krause informed the latest arrivals that many more transports were to come. A clean-up detail was formed to prepare additional houses, which had already been searched for valuables by Drechsler's aides.

From the veritable mountains of snow to be cleared away, it was apparent to all that workers were badly needed in the city; yet, the very next day, Krause selected 200 young men to go to Camp Salaspils, where they were to build even more barracks. There, they met the Jews from Jungfernhof.

On December 14, 1941 another transport arrived, this time from Duesseldorf. The trip from Duesseldorf to Riga had been interrupted by a series of untoward incidents. When the deportees had boarded the train, one of them, a man, had attempted to commit suicide, and one woman had made an unsuccessful attempt to escape. The placement of deportees on the trains had been done in a rather haphazard manner. In some cars there had been as many as sixty persons, while other cars had only thirty passengers. There had been heat in all twenty cars of the train at least at the outset of the journey. After passing through several stations, two of the cars had to be taken out of service because the axles had broken. One railroad agent in Konitz (Chojnice) had less sympathy for the German police accompanying the Jews than for their victims, but the personnel working at the station in Schaulen (Siauliai) turned off all the lights and shut off the heat in the cars in which the Jews were travelling.*

*A full account of the journey written by Captain Salitter in his secret report is given in translation in the appendix.

The official in charge of the transport, Captain Salitter of the *Schutzpolizei*, kept a record of temperatures during the journey and noted how cold it became the nearer they came to Riga. Once in Riga, he was under the impression that Skirotava, the name of the last stop in Riga, was also the name of the ghetto. He mentioned in his report that the Riga Ghetto at that time contained 2,500 Jewish males and that another 32,500 had been shot by the Latvians! His figures therefore tend to agree with those of Max Kaufmann and *Einsatzgruppe A,* and not with those given by Gerald Reitlinger.[19]

Conforming to the procedures established for all earlier transports and those which were yet to come, the deportees had to leave their luggage at Skirotava station. They were told that they would get their belongings at a later time, but they never saw them again. The luggage was taken to one of the many places in the city where the belongings of the Jews were sorted and assessed.

The new arrivals then walked into the ghetto, where a group elder and a man in charge of labor details were chosen. Several other men were appointed to act as the group's police force, called *Ordnungsdienst.*

On December 16, 1941, a contingent of Jews from Bielefeld and vicinity arrived. Again everything followed the same pattern, but there was one surprise that gladdened all the ghetto inmates. One of the young men who came from Bielefeld found his family in the ghetto. They had come from Cassel a few days before.[20]

Two days later, on December 18, a transport from Hanover arrived. The commandant selected as the elder for this group Guenther Fleischel, a Roman Catholic by religious persuasion. Rumor had it that Fleischel had first met Krause when he, Fleischel, had attempted to join the Nazi "Brown Shirts." But that had been before Fleischel had found out that his own father had been a Jew, and that he, too, was therefore subject to all of Hitler's anti-Jewish laws, including deportation. Still, Fleischel was a good-looking man, well over six feet tall, the type whom Germans thought of as a natural leader, and so he seemed to have established some kind of rapport with Krause, which appeared to give substance to the story that the two men had met somewhere before.

Shortly before his deportation, Fleischel had met a very beautiful young woman. In Riga, they entered into what was called a "ghetto marriage." In this arrangement, the woman took her partner's last name. Although the "marriage" could not be officially sanctioned, most of the ghetto inmates accepted this procedure, to the extent that even the administration offices of the various ghetto groups entered the woman's new name on their records. By this time, the ghetto already had a bureaucracy of its own.

In his capacity as a ghetto functionary—besides being a Roman Catholic—Fleischel regularly held Catholic services at his apartment. These services were attended by many of the other Catholics who had been deported to the ghetto because of their Jewish descent. These unfortunates who were Christians by religion but "Jews by race," were a marginal element in the ghetto, accepted neither by the Jews nor by the Germans.

Krause, who was a Catholic himself, knew about the church services at Fleischel's apartment. As for Fleischel's new wife, it was said that she never attended.

With the arrival of the group from Hanover, a new precedent was set: a woman was appointed to an official function in the ghetto. Selma Sollinger of Hanover was placed in charge of labor details for her group. Her husband, Julius, was assigned to the ghetto police force of eight appointed for the Hanover group. The Sollingers' daughter and son-in-law were assigned to work details outside the ghetto.

No more transports arrived in December 1941, obviously

because the trains were needed to return German soldiers home on furlough in time for Christmas.

On December 22, 1941, another 500 men were taken from the Riga Ghetto to Camp Salaspils, among them the young man from Bielefeld who had just found his family. After they left, there were about 4,000 German Jews and over 3,000 Latvian Jews in the two ghettos. Living conditions were difficult; all the water pipes had frozen, there was very little food, and that particular winter was one of the coldest on record. However, many of the people who went to work each day to places outside the ghetto, in the city itself, were able to barter their jewelry and clothing for food, and in this way to supplement their meager rations. They did this at the risk of severe punishment, even death, but their hunger was so great that they threw caution to the winds. Thus, hardly a day passed without a hanging, the most common form of punishment for men. Women were shot in the cemetery by Krause.

The hangings were gruesome; the victims lost control over the sphincter muscles, and the horrified audience was witness to this final indignity. At the end of that day, the columns of labor details were ordered to pass by the execution site and to watch the bodies sway in the icy air.

People were coughing and sneezing, their feet were swollen from hunger, they suffered from frostbite and diarrhea and, to make matters worse, there was little in the way of proper medication. A hospital was opened on the German side of Ludzas Iela, opposite the *Linas Hazedek* (which had been the hospital of the Latvian Jews) with Dr. Hans Aufrecht of the Cologne group in charge as medical superintendent.

The Cologne group, having been the first from Germany to arrive, was not only more favored in the way of power positions, but was also the only group in the German ghetto to have a small synagogue, not far from the cemetery. The ghetto elite worshipped there on Friday nights and on the High Holy Days. Most of the people, however, said their prayers either in the privacy of their own homes or in small groups at the home of someone able and willing to conduct services.

The ghetto had no rabbi. Dr. Joseph Carlebach, Chief-rabbi of Hamburg and Altona, was in Jungfernhof and did his best to ease the hard life of his flock there. He saw to it that the holidays were observed and that the *Kaddish* was recited in memory of the dead; he consoled the bereaved when loved ones died, and raised the morale of all those around him. He and part of his family were exterminated in March, 1942. After he was gone, there was little left of organized religious life, but people somehow knew the correct dates of the Jewish holidays and tried to observe them. Some observed the Jewish dietary laws at least to the extent of not eating pork.

In Camp Salaspils, a Hebrew teacher named Jaffee from Stuttgart, saw to it that, despite Nazi orders to the contary, *Kaddish* was recited at the mass burial site.[2 1]

Each group in the ghetto had several older men who carried out religious functions in addition to their regular jobs. They came from all walks of life, from many different cities and even different countries, but the bond that united them was their deep piety.

They kept track of the Jewish calendar, they prevailed upon the schoolteachers of their groups to make sure that the children would observe holidays, they hoarded candle stumps for Sabbath lights, and on Friday nights they could be heard welcoming the Sabbath into their poor, dilapidated domiciles. They performed the rituals connected with death and burial, and most of the time, Krause let them have their way with the bodies of those he had executed. He sometimes watched them saying their prayers over the open graves, but intent as they were on their sad duty, they hardly noticed him.

Shortly before Passover 1942, they sent a committee to Fleischel, the Hanover group elder, prevailing upon him to ask Commandant Krause for permission to bake *matzoth,* the unleavened bread which at another time and in another place had symbolized the end of slavery. Permission was granted and each person was to receive just one piece of *matzah,* more as a token than anything else. Those who observed Passover by not eating leavened bread, bartered their bread rations for potatoes.

While many applauded the efforts of these pious men and women, there were some who scoffed at the old traditions. Their own personal grief left no room for a belief in a higher power. Among them there were some who had been Orthodox in their former lives, but had now lost both faith and hope. The reverse happened, too. Men who, before the war had been Jews in name only turned to religion in an attempt to find meaning in their sufferings. Since their religious education was sketchy, they read the ancient Hebrew prayers haltingly, trying hard to keep pace with the tiny congregations.

Prayer books were scarce and had to be shared. They had either come from Germany, carried by the deportees on their persons, or they had been found in the houses, having been left there by the former occupants who had gone to their deaths. It was a foregone conclusion that each school in the ghetto should have at least one prayer book so that the pupils could learn the prayers.

Many of the Orthodox Jews were unwilling to make any compromise whatsoever in their strict observance of the dietary laws. Because there was no kosher meat available, they refused to eat any meat or food containing meat products, and thus they literally starved themselves to death. Many of them, weakened by hunger and hard labor, did not survive the first winter of the Riga Ghetto.

3
Life in the Ghetto

From the very beginning, life in the ghetto was disciplined and well ordered. Older women who could not go out to work were required to clean the houses, the courtyards, and some of the apartments as well, so that those who had outside jobs and came home exhausted after work, would be able to conserve their energies. Herbert Schultz, who was in overall charge of organizing labor details and was in constant touch with the German authorities, spread the word that the survival of the ghetto inmates depended on how much work they would be able to do for their Nazi overlords.

At that particular time, the work consisted of shoveling snow from the city's busy thoroughfares and of unloading cargo in the harbor. Women were also sent out to clean the quarters of the SS, army, and air force personnel stationed in Riga. People with special skills, such as mechanics, tool and die makers, watchmakers, and engravers, were made part of the more important German war machine. Since war-related work was often quite demanding, they were given food at their places of employment, obviously to keep them fit. These jobs were therefore considered desirable and added to the status of the person fortunate or skilled enough to obtain them.

Unfortunately, many of the German Jews had been merchants or members of the professions, and not artisans in Germany. As for the younger people, who could have learned crafts easily, they had been sent to Salaspils. It was therefore the Latvian Jews who ended up getting the better jobs, since many of them had been skilled workers before the war. This

35

meant that they were, economically speaking, in a far better position than their fellow Jews from Germany.

After a lapse of almost four weeks, additional transports of deportees reached Riga. On January 13, 1942, the first Czech Jews arrived via Theresienstadt.[22] Following its arrival in Riga, this new transport, given the name of "Prague group," was organized like all the groups that had come before. The street in the German ghetto where the Czech Jews were assigned living quarters was named "Prager Strasse;" at its end was the big gate to the Latvian ghetto which was guarded at all times by Jewish police from both ghettos.

Two days later, another 400 young men, among them many of the newly arrived Czech Jews, left the ghetto for Camp Salaspils. On the same day, a transport from Vienna arrived at Skirotava station, but this time the procedure was different. Only about 300 people from that contingent were marched into the Riga Ghetto. Since their number did not warrant the formation of a new group, the 300 Viennese were added to the Prague group. The other Viennese were sent directly to Jungfernhof.[23]

The next day brought a contingent of Jews from Berlin. Another street, the old Mazu Kalna Iela—actually only one side of it—was "opened" up, and was renamed Berliner Strasse. From this group, too, a woman, Mrs. Scheucher, was put in charge of labor details, but she could not put together many such details, because her transport contained a great many old people and children. Those able to work were immediately added to the labor details that went out every day. Private firms, in addition to the military installations, were clamoring for Jewish workers. They sent their own civilian employees to pick up the small Jewish labor details, and the ghetto authorities must have trusted them because they saw no need to send uniformed guards with the contingents.

By now there were many children in the ghetto and plans

were discussed for the establishment of schools. Guenther Fleischel, the elder of the Hanover group, approached Krause and was given permission to set up schools in every group. In addition to regular academic subjects, Krause ordered Ruth Wilner, a former dance instructor, to give the children gymnastics lessons once a week. He had heard about her from Schultz's assistant, Mr. Baum, whose son Ernst had been one of her pupils in Cologne. She was allowed to absent herself from her regular work one day each week, and was given the use of an empty hall in the house behind the *Kommandantur* (the main office building) for her classes. She taught the children on an hourly basis, for example, children from Cologne from 9:00 to 10:00 A.M., children from Cassel from 10:00 to 11:00 A.M., and so on.[24]

Krause had indicated to Fleischel that additional transports containing even more children were scheduled to arrive, but it was rather difficult to imagine where the newcomers would be housed, because the ghetto was bursting at its seams. While a directive from the *Generalkommissar* in Latvia ordered that four Jews be housed in each room, in reality there were often as many as ten and twelve, depending on the size of the room. It was therefore necessary to set up a system that would ensure the best possible utilization of every inch of space, one that would also ensure cleanliness and order, so that life could be made a little more bearable. To implement this system, one man called *Hauskommandant* (house commander), was placed in charge of each house. He was responsible for sanitary conditions and for delivering messages to the inhabitants of his house. He acted as a go-between transmitting orders that filtered down from the authorities, and saw to it that everyone obeyed them, such as getting the required permission from the doctor if one wanted to stay home from work. It was the *Hauskommandant* who personally assigned families to rooms so as to make sure that the allocation of space was fair. Before that position was created, newcomers had simply been told the number of persons each house was supposed to accommodate and were then expected to find their own locations and make the best of them.

Late at night on January 18, 1942, another transport arrived from Czechoslovakia. Eighty men from this transport were taken off the train that same evening and were sent to Camp Salaspils. The others were not unloaded until the morning, and were brought into the ghetto, where they were incorporated into the Prague group.[25] Since these new arrivals needed all the houses on Prager Strasse, most of the deportees from Vienna were moved to Berliner Strasse and were incorporated into the Berlin group. They were put into No. 2, the largest house on the street, as were people who came with the next transport from Berlin two days later. Most of the deportees were elderly people.

The apartments became very cramped. The proximity to one another, the lack of privacy, and their physical disabilities, made the older people especially, very irritable. Arguments broke out from real and imaginary causes, and life, already difficult enough, became even worse.

By the time the next transport arrived, one week later, on January 25, 1942, the clean-up work detail had taken care of the entire street which divided the two ghettos. Inasmuch as the new contingent came from Saxony, bringing Jews from Leipzig and Dresden, Ludzas Iela was renamed "Leipziger Strasse." On this street, in addition to the *Kommandantur*, where the commandant had his offices, there were the headquarters of the police, both German and Jewish, the offices of Schultz, containing all records relating to the various work details, and the big warehouse to which food was delivered for distribution to the various groups.

Even though the houses had been cleaned, the newcomers from Saxony found food left by the former occupants on the tables. The food had frozen solid, but after it was thawed, it turned out to be still edible and therefore precious. They found clothing as well; this, too, was welcome.

On January 30, another transport arrived from Berlin, and a few hours later a contingent came in from Vienna. A new "Vienna group" was created and assigned to the other side of Berliner Strasse, as well as to several houses facing the barbed-wire fence that separated the ghetto from the outside world. They called this short street "Moskauer Strasse," even though the real Moskavas Iela, one of the main roads in Riga, was the next parallel street at that particular point. The inmates were not allowed to use the doors leading to the outside, but only the back doors opening into the courtyards behind the houses. The clean-up detail had not been ordered to work there as yet, so that the new arrivals found not only frozen food and clothing, but several dead bodies as well.

On the next morning, Mr. Karl Loebl was appointed elder of the new Vienna group, and Mrs. Else Sekules was placed in charge of the group's labor details. Several men were assigned to the ghetto police.

On February 1, 1942, a contingent from Dortmund arrived and was formed into a group exactly like the others preceding it. By then, everyone thought that no more transports would be coming.[26] The clean-up details were not abolished, but they were told that there would be no more newcomers and so the guards let them make firewood from some furniture in the houses where they worked.[27]

Even after the incorporation of additional houses, the German ghetto was extremely overcrowded. Each room held so many people that it was impossible to avoid stumbling over one's neighbor during the night when the mattresses were placed on the floor. During the day the mattresses were pushed flat against the wall to create more space. Whatever there was of furniture soon became firewood for cooking.

On February 3, about twenty members of the German Jewish ghetto police were taken to the forest where they were ordered to dig graves, using dynamite because the ground was frozen. After they had completed their task, they were brought back into the ghetto and were forbidden, under the threat of death, to tell anyone, even their families, where they had been and what they had done.[28]

On Thursday, February 5, 1942, members of the Berlin and Vienna groups were instructed not to go to work but to assemble in front of their houses right on Berliner Strasse. Together, the two groups numbered well over 4,000. The street was teeming with SS men. The Jewish men in charge of the houses were instructed to have everyone come out, even the sick. The officer in charge was Lange's deputy, Gerhard Maywald. He took his position in front of No. 2 Berliner Strasse and ordered the Jews to file past him.

Meanwhile, several SS men went into the houses to ascertain whether anyone was hiding inside. They found several people and ordered them to get out but did not use their guns against them. They behaved with restraint; obviously, they had been ordered not to alarm the inmates in any way.

As the people filed past *Obersturmfuehrer* Maywald, he asked each of them politely whether he or she was working, and if so, where. Those who gave affirmative replies were told to go home; in many cases the presence of even one worker in a family was enough to cause the dismissal of the entire family. Those who were too sick or too old to work and had no one to vouch for them, were told that they were being sent to a camp in Duenamuende, where they would be given some easy work to do. They were loaded onto trucks waiting at the corner of Berliner Strasse and Leipziger Strasse. In several cases, for no apparent reason, even young people were included, such as Mrs. Anna Sauerquell, a strikingly beautiful, statuesque women from Vienna, who had been in the ghetto only five days and had not as yet been assigned to work, because her son Kurt was sick with a sore throat. Maywald asked her what work she had done in Vienna, and she answered that she had been a nurse in a home for the aged. "Very good," Maywald said, "Then you can go along and take care of the old people here, too." When her son, fourteen years old, six feet tall, and good looking like his mother, wanted to go with her, Maywald did not allow him to go along. The boy did not go back into his house but hung around to see whether he would somehow be able to join his mother without being noticed by Maywald. He made his way up the length of Berliner Strasse, behind the houses, almost to the corner where the trucks were waiting. From there, he could see that the people were being thrown into the trucks if they were unable to board them on their own. As the trucks left, he could see legs hanging out, and the sight, of course, filled him with dread.[29]

Only those twenty Jewish policemen who had prepared the mass graves two days earlier knew what was about to happen. They knew that the people on the trucks were going to join the Latvian Jews who had been killed in the forest earlier.

Altogether, approximately 1,500 Jews—about 1,100 from Berlin and 400 from Vienna—were taken out of the ghetto that day. Other groups in the ghetto were not involved; the reason for this strictly localized "operation" evidently stemmed from the fact that the Berlin group had supplied only a small number of workers. Because the Viennese happened to be living on the same street, logistics decreed that they should be included in the "operation."

While many of those who remained behind had misgivings, the absence of a distinctive pattern allowed for some hope that no harm had befallen the others. After all, younger people had been taken away, too, and many of the older people had been permitted to stay with their families, provided one family member was working. It is true that most of those who had been taken away had been unfit for work, but the optimists did believe that these unfortunates had merely been transferred to another camp, where the work was indoors and easier.

This optimism seemed to be borne out three days later, when 200 women, who up to then had been inmates of Camp Jungfernhof, arrived in the ghetto. Most of them were from Hamburg, and they were added to the Hanover group. They brought news of many who had been taken to Jungfernhof and had not been heard from since. Little did these women realize that the days of most of the Jungfernhof inmates were numbered. In fact, the very day after the women had left, an "operation" similar to that in the ghetto, had taken place at Jungfernhof, and approximately 1,000 had been taken from the camp to their deaths.

On February 10, 1942, another contingent arrived from Vienna. It was to be the last one to reach the ghetto, and was met at Skirotava Station by Lange and the ubiquitous Maywald. Lange had last been seen on January 13, when he had put in an appearance to meet the first transport from Czechoslovakia. His long vacation, during which he attended the Wannsee Conference had not changed him at all. Even though he was somewhat smaller and darker than the blond, blue-eyed Maywald, he looked very handsome in his fur-collared uniform coat and seemed every inch an officer and a gentleman. It never occurred to the newcomers to suspect such a man of being a murderer.

Lange told these latest arrivals that those who were unwilling or unable to walk the seven kilometers to the ghetto could make the trip on trucks that had been especially reserved for them. "In this way," he said, "those of you who ride can prepare a place for those who walk." It was an extremely cold day—forty-two degrees below zero to be exact—and so the majority of the hapless, unsuspecting Jews from Vienna took his advice and lined up to board the trucks. They did not know that those grayish-blue trucks had been manufactured by the Saurer Works in Austria especially for the implementation of the Final Solution. These trucks were the famous gas vans, which were used from time to time despite the fact that the SS did not especially like them because they always had mechanical problems.

My father, my mother, my sister, and I were among the latest arrivals. My sister Rita, then eleven years old, wanted to go by truck, but my father told her that families should stay together. When she became obstinate and began to whine, my father, in a rare show of temper, slapped her. Lange turned around, gave her a stern look, and told her that children should always listen to their parents. A few months later, Lange saw my father in the ghetto and, in a flash of recognition, asked him whether his family was still staying together.

Approximately 300 had chosen to walk and thus reached the ghetto, where they were incorporated into the Vienna group. Two corpses were unloaded from the train; one man had died of a heart attack en route, and the other man, the well-known financier Siegmund Bosel, had been shot during the trip by transport commander Alois Brunner. Bosel had been brought to the train at Vienna's Aspang Station directly from a hospital, by ambulance. According to rumors, he had already been safe in England but had been called back to Vienna to untangle some of his complicated financial affairs. He had been promised safe conduct, but the SS betrayed him; and he was added to the transport just before it left Vienna on February 6, 1942.

During the second night of the trip, Alois Brunner chained Bosel, still in his pajamas, to the platform of the first car, and berated him for having been a profiteer. The old man repeatedly asked for mercy; he was very ill, and it was bitterly cold. Finally, Brunner wearied of the game and shot him. Afterwards Brunner walked into the car and asked whether anyone had heard anything. After being assured that no one had, he seemed satisfied and left.

The new arrivals were told by the ghetto "old-timers" that their friends and relatives who had decided to ride in the trucks had probably been taken to one of the camps in the vicinity. Again, this explanation sounded credible because earlier arrivals could point to the fact that they had just heard from relatives who had been separated from them in the same manner at the station. Other rumors were too terrible to be believed. Sometimes Latvian civilians or even German military personnel would talk about what was going on in the forest outside the city. The Latvian Jews who had witnessed much of the killing, believed all the reports and had no illusions about their own chances, but the German Jews remained curiously oblivious to the truth. Some of them had doubts, of course, but these were dispelled by incidents such as the encounter of Lange and the disobedient child. A man who talked like that to a little girl could not be capable of mass murder. One merely assumed that many of the horror stories were greatly exaggerated or that such things happened mainly to East European Jews, not to Jews from the Reich. Somehow, even then, the Jews from Germany still adhered to the illusion that they were better than the *Ostjuden* from Latvia.

At one point, when the people at the station who had chosen to make the last leg of the journey on foot milled around, waiting for some signal to be given, Dr. Lange called out to them, *"Ihr bloedes Volk, kommt 'mal her!"* (Come here, you stupid people!) The arrivals did not invest his words with any ominous meaning. In retrospect, Lange may really have considered them stupid, since he had been able to dupe them so easily. He most probably shared the opinion of the German Minister for Propaganda. Dr. Joseph Goebbels, who asserted in his diary that the Jews were not as smart as they liked to think. "When they are in danger," he wrote, "they prove to be the stupidest devils."[30]

Altogether then, twenty transports of Jews, totalling

exactly 20,057 people, had reached Riga. This figure agrees with the reports made by the *Einsatzgruppe* and also with Kaufmann's estimate. Reitlinger, underestimating as usual, maintained that "a figure of 15,000 for all the Riga transports, including the death transports, might be rather high." His dates for the transports are incorrect; he omitted some, and he misinterpreted *Einsatzgruppe* leader Franz Stahlecker's report that half of the Jews had been admitted to the Riga Ghetto and half to two labor camps. Stahlecker was referring to Camp Jungfernhof and Camp Salaspils; he was essentially correct. The only transport to go straight to the forest was the one from Berlin, which had arrived on November 30, 1941. There were others, which would come later and whose "passengers" would pass through Salaspils on the way to be murdered in the forest.

In the meantime, as of February 10, 1942, there were approximately 2,500 Jews in Jungfernhof, 11,000 Jews in the German ghetto, 3,500 men and 300 women in the Latvian ghetto, and another 1,300 men in Salaspils. The reason for the small number of men in Salaspils was that the death rate there was the highest of all the camps. New groups of German and Czech Jews were continuously taken from the ghetto to Salaspils. At first, only young, single people went, but eventually even older, family men shared the same fate.

In addition to Jews working at the main camps, there were small groups of Jews employed at several places in the city, sorting the clothes of those who had died and packing them for shipment to Germany. Others, mainly Latvian Jews, were employed in factories whose managers found it easier, and perhaps safer not to let them return to the ghetto each night but to keep them at their places of work. In this way, the management could be sure of their labor supply and saved time by not having to bring the Jews to and from the ghetto each day.

Thus, of the 20,057 Jews from the Reich who had come to

Riga, almost 15,000 were still alive at this point: Even from a historical perspective, the odds for the survivors did not seem too bad. As for the inmates of the German ghetto, they did not know that one-fourth of their number had already been exterminated. To them it was clear that they had been "re-settled" as forced laborers, and they were able to live with that idea. Accordingly, they hoped that their strength would last until the war was over; they settled down in the ghetto and began to regard it as their home.

4
Winter: 1941-1942

The German part of the Riga Ghetto consisted of ten groups, organized mainly by city of origin. These groups, in order of their arrival, were: Cologne, Cassel, Duesseldorf, Bielefeld, Hanover, Prague, Berlin, Leipzig, Vienna, and Dortmund. Each group had as its leader a group elder, who frequently had another man as his assistant. Each group also had been assigned one person to take charge of the labor details, and an office where the elder and the labor administrators kept their records and did their work.

Leiser of the Cologne group, who held the title of "ghetto elder," was the boss of all the group elders, and Schultz was the head of all the labor detail administrators. Schultz actually dealt directly with the outside world, both German and Latvian. He had two assistants, Schiff and Baum, as well as three or four secretaries. The ghetto administration was responsible to the *Reichssicherheitshauptamt* (Reich Security Headquarters, RSHA for short) which was run in a military fashion.

As the ghetto grew, so did its bureaucracy; the German authorities insisted on detailed reports, which, for lack of typewriters, were written out by hand at the groups' offices and were delivered to the *Kommandantur* by 11:30 each morning by the *Ordonnanz* (messenger) of the group. These communications were equivalent to "morning reports" in the army. They contained the following information: the number of people in the group as of that day, the names of those who had died during the night, how many were out sick for the day, how many were employed at jobs within the ghetto, the

47

number of children, and the number of people who had gone to work on jobs outside the ghetto. At the main office, the reports were then tallied against the lists of the outgoing labor details made by Baum and Schiff earlier that day.

The *Kommandantur* housed both the central office for work administration, which was later moved further up on Leipziger Strasse, and the offices of the commandant of the ghetto, at that time Kurt Krause. Krause had a Jewish secretary who in turn had several assistants working for her.

Krause came in every day and kept his eyes on everything. Because the ghetto administration received wages for the workers sent out each day, records had to be kept. All of them required the commandant's signature; income as well as expenses for food had to be accounted for.

Each group had its own small store where the daily rations were given out. These "local" foodstores received their supplies from the central food warehouse on Leipziger Strasse. Two people usually worked in each store; they had a list of names of everyone in their particular group, and they checked off the names of those who came in and received their food. Generally, workers on jobs within the ghetto picked up rations for those who toiled outside, in order to spare them the task. There was hardly any cheating since people knew one another and depended very much on one another. Such behavior as stealing food would have meant ostracism; besides, it would have been in conflict with the middle-class mores which prevailed in the ghetto.

The ghetto also had a *Kleiderkammer,* or clothing center, a large warehouse where inmates, upon presentation of an official order to the effect that they were in dire need of apparel, could procure shoes and clothes. Such as order could be obtained from the group's elder and was usually not too difficult to get. Of course, the better acquainted an inmate was with his elder, the better was his chance to obtain such an order. It was therefore a good idea to bring the elder a box of cigarettes from time to time or a special tidbit from the outside. This attitude was expressed by the old saying, "If you don't grease the wheels, the cart won't move."

The clothes and shoes available to the people in the ghetto were those considered too shabby to be sent to the Reich. For the ghetto, however, they constituted an important part of the economy, for besides functioning as wearing apparel, they were used for barter outside the ghetto. The staff of the clothing center consisted of women from Cologne, Cassel, and Hanover. These women took some of the clothing home with them and passed it on to their "connections," people who would barter the articles outside the ghetto and then share the proceeds with them on a fifty-fifty basis. Naturally, the women were careful to set aside only the best clothing for this purpose because there was no market for really inferior goods. If one was wise and did not come to the clothing center empty-handed, one's chances for getting relatively good clothes were that much better.

Each group had at least one doctor, and there were a number of dentists in the ghetto. There was also the hospital, euphemistically called *Zentral Lazarett;* there, Dr. Hans Aufrecht of Cologne, the ghetto's medical superintendent, had his office. The physicians who did most of the work were Dr. Josef, a gynecologist, and Dr. Mintz, the internist who had treated Lenin. Both doctors were members of the Latvian ghetto, even though Dr. Josef had originally fled from Germany and was well known to some of his former compatriots.

The most commonly performed operations were abortions. In the first year, there were a few normal births, but the babies were immediately put to death by an injection of poison. The mothers were told that their infants had been stillborn. One baby boy, born to a Latvian Jewess, survived for a while, but he, too, was eventually put to death. He had been named Ben Ghetto—Son of the Ghetto.

As medical superintendent, Dr. Aufrecht performed yet another function. If an inmate was assigned to a *Kommando* which he did not like but from which he could not be transferred because he was performing some specialized job considered vital to the war effort, only Aufrecht could determine that due to some illness or infirmity, he should be transferred to another labor detail. Aufrecht tried his best to accommodate those who sought his help in obtaining transfers, but he was not popular in the ghetto. Most people thought him arrogant. This impression was reinforced by the fact that he hardly ever greeted anyone in the street. Actually, this was not voluntary; he was extremely nearsighted, even when he wore his glasses, and therefore he rarely recognized people. Few, if any, realized the pressures under which Aufrecht was working. Ghetto Commandant Krause visited the hospital almost every day; it was he who disposed of the few babies born in the ghetto. In addition, Krause always exhorted hospital patients to "get up and work! The ghetto needs only healthy people."

Young women who had to undergo abortions made Krause especially angry. To the discomfiture of patients and doctors alike, the commandant sometimes even insisted on staying to watch the operation.[31]

It was for this reason that eventually the Jewish authorities, prodded by Dr. Aufrecht, set up a secret operating room in one of the houses belonging to the Cassel group. Most of the abortions were performed there to make sure that Krause would not learn of them and carry out his threat to have the father and mother sterilized for the "crime" of having attempted to produce a child in the ghetto.

There were several nurses in the hospital, headed by Dr. Aufrecht's wife who once had worked as a nurse herself. She also took charge of the secret operating room in the Cassel group.

The hospital had a so-called welfare office, where a Mrs.

Rosenthal, from Cologne, tried to aid those ghetto inmates who had absolutely no resources except their rations, or who needed help for a variety of reasons but were too proud or bashful to ask for anything. She contacted people who were known to bring in great quantities of food from the outside and persuaded them to give up some of it; she then brought the food to the needy. There was a kitchen in the hospital, where she had soup prepared. She then enlisted the help of ghetto police and messengers to carry the soup in army containers to her charges. It was not much, but it was something. Mrs. Rosenthal was a very pious woman who considered her work not only necessary but highly ethical. There were those, of course, who envied her this job. The fact that she was quite heavy gave rise to many jokes about the food she collected. After the liquidation of the ghetto in November 1943, when she arrived at Camp Kaiserwald, people who never realized that she had been truly devoted to the welfare of the poor, taunted her and waited for her fat to melt away. Some months later, when she died at one of the camps attached to Kaiserwald, she was still rather heavy.

Each group in the German ghetto had its own police force. At first, their number depended on the size of the group. Thus, Hanover at one point had eight policemen, while Vienna had four. Eventually, there was a total staff of forty. The head of the German ghetto police was Rudolf Haar, from the Cologne group. His men wore dark coats, riding breeches, boots, army type peaked caps, and armbands on the left arm with the name of their group. Such armbands were worn also by all other ghetto personnel to provide instant identification. In addition, of course, the German Jews wore the yellow Star of David on their chests with the word *Jude* in German lettering, designed to resemble Hebrew script. The Latvian Jews had to wear two stars, without any inscription, one in front and one in back. This made it virtually impossible for them to disappear in a crowd when bartering valuables for food outside the ghetto. When the German Jews on their way to Riga had first noticed the double insignia, they had not understood the reason for this special mark of identification. Later they realized that it made good sense, at least from the point of view of the Nazi authorities.

Good organization permitted both ghettos to function smoothly. Except for the periodic incidents at the hospital that involved Krause, there was little interference from the SS. The Nazis were convinced and with good reason, that the inmates were doing their best to obey regulations in order to keep things on an even keel and not "make waves." The various SS officers even felt secure enough to walk about freely in the German ghetto. They were a common sight, known by name, and whoever passed by them in the streets snapped to attention and then moved on. The only SS officer everyone feared and hated was Lange. He had discarded the role of courteous officer who greeted the transports at the station; his appearance in the ghetto brought on panic every time. The streets emptied as soon as the Jewish police, or the *Ordonnanz* gave warning that Lange was around. On several occasions he simply gunned down people who in his opinion walked too slowly. He shot Jews at random just because they happened to be in his path. The nationality of his victims was a matter of indifference to him; he shot German and Latvian Jews with equal zest. To the other SS men, however, the nationality of the Jews might have mattered, for they seldom, if ever, walked through the Latvian ghetto as they did through the German area. If they did go into the Latvian ghetto, it was strictly on business and always in groups.

Krause, who never missed a day of work in the ghetto, often stopped ghetto inmates and asked them questions. At one time, in late March, 1942, he walked up to my mother, who was coming home from work, and asked her what she had in her coat pocket; he could see a bottle protruding. She took out the bottle and showed him that it contained milk.

She then produced a sandwich from her other pocket, telling Krause that a Latvian civilian had given her these goodies while she had been out shoveling snow. She added that they would be a great treat for her two little girls. The unpredictable Krause, who had killed people for much lesser "crimes," merely replied, "Funny, you people always get presents, but nobody gives me anything!" and told her to go home. She was a nervous wreck by the time she got there.

Incidents such as this were common. Had my mother run afoul of Krause in one of his "killing" moods, he would have marched her off to the cemetery to be shot. But unlike Lange, Krause never shot people at random. He had a legalistic mind; there had to be some sort of "crime," which he would consider reason enough for extreme punishment. It was far better not to cower before him; he hated to have someone cry or beg for mercy.

Announcements or orders from the Nazi authorities were communicated to the ghetto inmates through the central ghetto administration, headed by ghetto elder Leiser and labor detail administrator Schultz. From their offices, the information was passed on by messengers to the offices of the various groups. These offices, in turn, sent their own messengers to inform the house commanders. Every evening, after the tired inmates had come home for the night, these house commanders would go from apartment to apartment, reading out the orders of the day. Orders mainly concerned changes in labor details; sometimes they referred to sanitation or hygiene; other announcements involved food rations.

The ghetto bureaucracy employed many people, and it worked efficiently. It was used for sinister purposes as well, such as when the German authorities decided that the ghetto was becoming far too crowded again and that there were too many people eating but not enough producing. Thus, in the early spring of 1942, each group in the ghetto was ordered to turn over to the *Kommandantur* a quota of between 60 and

120 persons for further "resettlement." The Berlin group was ordered to supply 600. On Saturday, March 14, 1942, the men and women in charge of labor detail administration compiled lists of names which the messengers of the various groups took to the house commanders. The Jewish ghetto administrators were told that the people selected in this way were to go to a labor detail outside the ghetto, in the city of Duenamuende, where they would be working in fish canneries. It was the same deception that had been used on February 5 in connection with the Berlin and Vienna groups. The author of the idea was Maywald. He boasted of it during his trial in 1977.

To the Jews the plan sounded credible. The Baltic Sea was rich in fish, and everyone knew that workers were badly needed everywhere. To the hungry old people who were ordered to go to Duenamuende, the magic words "fish canneries" implied food as well as a certain security and reprieve from the cold. While most of those selected for this work were elderly or ailing or parents with small children, some of the ghetto functionaries were chosen as well. A number of physicians were also put on the lists, ostensibly to take care of workers who might get sick.

The elder of the Vienna group, Mr. Loebl, was to go along too, together with his daughter Inge. Her feet had been amputated shortly after the Loebls had reached the ghetto. The railroad car in which they had made the journey from Vienna to Riga had not been heated; as a result, Inge had suffered severe frostbite which ended in gangrene. Her father was to become the elder in charge of the new camp to which they were going. There was nothing to fear. In other groups, similar arrangements were made; some of the administrative personnel were added to the lists to assist Loebl in Camp Duenamuende and to make sure that the new camp would operate smoothly right from the start.

A look at any map would have been enough to ascertain

that even the name "Duenamuende" was fictitious. It meant mouth of the Duena and had a ring of truth to it, for there was a city called Duenaburg. But Duenamuende? Unfortunately, no one thought of checking any maps. Thus, Maywald's invention was a great success.

The people who were to leave busied themselves with packing the few belongings they still owned. Valuables, such as watches and other jewelry which they had kept in defiance of orders to turn these items over to the Germans, were sewn into their clothing. Staple foods, such as flour, sugar, and fats, were transformed into baked goods so that they could be transported more easily. There was an air of real excitement in the ghetto. It seemed that everyone remained up half that night, either getting ready to leave themselves, or helping those who had been "chosen" to go.

On Sunday morning, those scheduled to leave assembled in front of their houses. From each group they moved slowly toward Leipziger Strasse, where trucks were waiting for them. Many who were not on the lists asked whether they could go along with their friends or relatives. Permission was readily granted. Others, however, who in the meantime had begun to have second thoughts on the matter, went into hiding. Because the required number of people seemed to be present, the German authorities did not check their lists to see whether anyone was missing, nor did they institute searches.

Toward the afternoon, after the last columns of the Berlin and Vienna groups had been waiting for hours, the SS men, evidently tired, became nasty. Mr. Nadel, the house commander of No. 13 Berliner Strasse, who had been assigned to go with the transport, received a rough shove because he tried to go back into the house with his little boy who wanted to use the toilet. When the child, who happened to be blond and blue-eyed, started to cry, the SS man relented and let them both go in. He waited for them outside, and when they emerged, he asked the boy his name and age. The child gave him the stock reply that he had probably picked up from some grownup, *"Rudi Nadel, drei Jahre, ledig und gesund!"* (Rudy Nadel, age three, single, and in good health!) The SS man laughed, gave him a piece of candy, and then urged father and son to get back into line so as not to miss the truck. The operation continued without a hitch.

The same procedure was also used at Camp Jungfernhof eleven days later, on March 26, 1942. Here, too, the people who had been "chosen" to go to Duenamuende left quite willingly because they had been promised easy indoor jobs and probably better food at their new place of work. But when some of the young people wanted to go along with their parents, *Oberscharfuehrer* Seck, the commandant of Jungfernhof, refused to give them permission to do so. Gerda Rose, a young girl, went down on her knees, begging to be allowed to go along with her mother and little brother. Seck just smiled at her, said something about how pretty she was, and refused her pleas.[32] To many of the inmates, his behavior seemed ominous, but for those already loaded upon the trucks, such second thoughts came much too late.

On that day, the population of Camp Jungfernhof was reduced by 1,840 persons. Because of the previous "selection" in the second week of February and the many natural deaths that had occurred during the first few weeks, the camp now had a total population of 450 men and women; this number remained constant, except for minor changes, until the summer of 1944.

The Riga Ghetto had lost approximately 1,900 people on that Sunday in March. The original quota requested by the Germans for "resettlement" to Duenamuende had been only 1,500,[33] apparently an amount that could be handled most efficiently by the busy *Sonderkommando*. But more than 400 additional people, whose names had not appeared on the lists, had been "resettled" with the others, because they themselves had asked to be included in the Duenamuende transport,[34] thinking that they would be better off in the new camp where they really hoped to find easier living and working conditions.

The Latvian Gentiles were well aware of what had happened in the ghetto and in the surrounding camps; they also knew that the trucks were not going to a labor camp but to the forest. An item quoted in *Daugavas Vanagi* (report of war-crimes trial procedings in Latvia after the war) mentions the account of a witness in Riga, who lived near Bikernieker Forest at the time and who had counted the trucks that rolled past her house the Friday and Saturday before Easter of 1942. She was obviously referring to the "operation" at Camp Jungfernhof. In her deposition she said that she counted forty-one trucks between morning and noon on that Friday alone.[35]

The aftermath of the resettlement operation may have been arranged purposely or perhaps it was accidental. On Monday and Tuesday, March 16 and 17, 1942, several trucks rolled into the ghetto and were unloaded. Their cargo was an assortment of personal effects of the people who had been resettled. There were clothes that had been taken off hurriedly by their owners—still turned inside out—stockings attached to girdles and shoes encrusted with mud. The trucks also yielded nursing bottles, children's toys, eyeglasses, bags filled with food, and satchels containing photographs and documents. All the cargo was dumped out at what was called the *Gewerbebetrieb*, a factory type of building located at the edge of the last houses of the Prague group and Tin Square, an open area used for a variety of purposes, notably public executions.

Each group in the ghetto was asked to send five women to this *Gewerbebetrieb* to help sort the clothes that had been unloaded from the trucks. The best items were to be shipped to Germany; the others were to be sent to the ghetto's own clothing center for distribution among the inmates. The women were not even told to keep quiet about their work or about what they found. They recognized many of the clothes, some by the names that had been sewn into them, some by the identity cards still in the pockets, and there were, of course, dresses, coats, and suits which they had seen on their friends and neighbors when they had left the ghetto only a few days before. The women also found jewelry and foreign currency, but it was difficult to smuggle these items out of the building, since several SS men watched, and there was an occasional search. Some of the women, however, were bold enough to take the chance and took with them some badly needed items for bartering.

Soon everyone in the ghetto knew about the cargo that the trucks had brought and about the condition of the clothes. It did not take any great imagination to understand what had happened to their owners. No longer did anyone scoff at the tales of the Latvian Jews nor think that this could happen only to *Ostjuden* and never to Jews from Germany. In many houses in the ghetto, *Kaddish,* the Hebrew prayer for the dead, was recited. The German ghetto was plunged into despair.

But despite their deep sorrow, there were Jews who rationalized that as long as a person was strong and able to work, he was in little danger; that as long as he was of use to the Germans, he would not become a victim. Others, however, gave up all hope and collapsed; within a few days, by the end of March, there were several attempted and successful suicides, the first since the arrival of the last transport.

Suicides usually occurred immediately after arrival in the ghetto rather than sometime after the person had become accustomed to prevailing conditions. Means of suicide varied. The means most frequently used was poison, such as an overdose of sleeping pills brought from home. In some cases, the death struggle took several days, as with Schlesinger, who had been a banker in Vienna, and his secretary. They had arrived in Riga with the transport of February 10, and both took sleeping pills that same night. The other occupants of the kitchen, which had been allotted to Schlesinger and the young lady, called Dr. Bloch, the group's doctor, who gave them black coffee as an antidote, but Bloch was sorry that he had attempted to save them, for he only prolonged their agony. It took them four days to die.

Several people jumped out of windows; some slashed their wrists and quietly bled to death. One family simply sat down in their courtyard one cold night, and holding each other tightly, allowed themselves to freeze to death.

There were two more small transports which subsequently left the ghetto. They consisted of males only and arrived safely at Camp Salaspils. The ghetto inmates were aware that life at Salaspils was extremely harsh and that conditions there were bad, but they also knew that the men had not been taken away from the ghetto for immediate extermination. Jews who held positions in the Salaspils hierarchy were able to visit the ghetto from time to time and brought news.

These two transports were to be the last to leave the ghetto for Salaspils. The first one left on April 2, and the second one left on May 4, 1942, both over the objections of Krause. There had been a long correspondence between the ghetto commandant and Lange, in which the latter stated that he needed many more men for work in the Salaspils peat bogs. Krause, on the other hand, insisted that he had to keep every available man for work in the city. Eventually a compromise was reached, and the last 300 men from Riga were "released" for work in Camp Salaspils.[36]

About one-third of these last two shipments, along with survivors from earlier transports to Salaspils, returned to the ghetto within the next few months. The last contingent, numbering 192, came back on August 2, 1942.[37] Many of the returnees died shortly after their arrival back in Riga; they were simply too far gone to recover their strength.

By the late summer of 1942, Salaspils had become primarily a camp for Latvian political prisoners and Russian prisoners of war. It also served as a transit center for a few subsequent Jewish transports on their journey to death in the forest. In addition to the Latvian and Russian men, the camp also had a barrack for children. From some depositions made by former inmates, and the reports contained in the secondary literature on the camp, which has been kept by the Soviet Republic of Latvia as a memorial, it appears that these children were used for medical experiments. Postwar examinations of exhumed bodies revealed that various poisons had been tested on the little victims. Tags worn by the children were found in the forest and at Salaspils. In many cases the tags were marked *"ohne Eltern"* (without parents), thus identifying the children as orphans. While many of the names on the tags were Jewish, there were many of Slavic origin also. Some of the transports had come from as far away as France. Most came from the Reich, but there were some from Belorussia and several from Czechoslovakia.[38]

Throughout 1942, vague rumors circulated through the ghetto that Jews were being brought to Riga and its environs for extermination. Ghetto inmates who were employed at what was called labor detail *Einsatzgruppe 2C,* which was in the city and kept its workers overnight instead of permitting them to return to the ghetto after working hours, knew the truth because they had been given a continuous flow of clothing and jewelry to sort out. From names and addresses carefully lettered on suitcases, these people could tell where the loot had originated. In addition to "packaged" articles, they also received "loose" shipments from towns all over Latvia, where Jews or Latvians had been executed. The personal effects of the dead, piled haphazardly onto trucks, were then brought to Riga for processing.

In this manner, news reached the ghetto of the razing of the village of Audrini because its inhabitants had harbored partisans. The officer in charge of this "operation"—the Latvian Lidice—was Captain Boleslaw Maikowskis, another of those Latvians who had eagerly joined the German SS.[39]

Before the good clothing and especially the jewelry were shipped to the Reich, the local SS brass had their pick. The Jewish women who cleaned the apartments of high SS officials were sometimes flabbergasted by the riches they found there: whole drawers full of rings and watches, closets filled with furs still bearing labels, and an abundance of other precious items.

There was yet another small group that knew the sad truth before all the others. This was a labor detail made up of thirty-eight Jewish men who were kept at the Central Prison and who were regularly taken to the forest to bury the victims. While they were in their cells at the prison, a record was played two hours each day, warning them never to talk about what they were doing. Of these thirty-eight men, only sixteen eventually came back to the ghetto, broken in body and spirit.

Even though several of these men risked death by telling their families and friends about what they had done, predicting that the same fate lay in store for them all, people just could not imagine that this would be their end. Their preoccupation with survival, their will and hope to live, left no room for such thoughts. The grim reality was unacceptable. People lived through one day at a time and rationalized that if they could keep on doing that, they would be able to hold out. They took such comfort as there was from the thought that there was nothing they could have done to help those who had been taken away, and from the fact that, following "Operation Duenamuende," things soon returned to normal in the ghetto. Besides, the winter was almost over now and they were still alive; this in itself seemed a good reason for a more optimistic outlook.

5
Spring: A Time for Hope

As the winter's snow and ice melted away, living conditions in the ghetto improved considerably. All winter long, the people had to haul their water from the ghetto's central well on Tin Square, right underneath the gallows. Half the precious water obtained from that dreary place would be spilled on the way back to one's home, freezing instantly on the cold pavement and making the streets slick and unsafe. But now the faucets in the houses of the ghetto began to work again, much to the satisfaction of those who lived there.

However, the long-awaited thaw also brought a new problem: The cesspools of the houses started to run over. Fearful of epidemics, the ghetto authorities enacted strict sanitary regulations to prevent the outbreak of disease. Each group was assigned its own inspector, an inmate who was excused from his other tasks to work full time on checking every house in his domain. It became an unwritten law that anyone considered guilty of a minor infraction of ghetto regulations would have to clean out the cesspools after coming home from work. These infractions included tardiness or laziness at work in the case of adults and truancy in the case of children. Until that time, such violations of ghetto regulations had either been ignored or had been punished by having the offender clean the streets.

Most of the time, however, there were no cases involving punishable violations; therefore, the inmates volunteered to take turns cleaning the cesspool of the houses in which they lived. The contents of the cesspools were either shoveled into

63

deep pits or used to fertilize the vacant lots behind the houses. Although the stench was unbearable at times, the ground thus treated became extremely fertile, yielding unbelievable harvests of vegetables after the summer. The seeds were obtained through barter in the city or even from German guards and administrators. The deep pits were filled and closed again; there was work to be done at all times. Younger men, if they had the strength, would do the work for their older relatives or for someone who could give them food in return for their services. It was fortunate that the thaw did not last too long, for the physical strain that it imposed on the ghetto population was enormous.

The terrible overcrowding had been somewhat alleviated by the "resettlement" of the ghetto's "excess" population in Operation Duenamuende of March 15; the people in the ghetto now had more space in which to move around. This, in turn, reduced friction and restored a semblance of normalcy to daily life. Furthermore, most of the workers no longer had to work in different places each day. Since the employers had official contracts with the Nazi ghetto authorities, they were in a position to insist on getting only trained personnel. People now knew exactly where they would be going to work every day. They met every morning at the same street corner, mainly on Prager Strasse where the columns lined up. They knew the precise time; it was always the same labor detail, they always worked with the same people, and in this way, their lives assumed a degree of stability. They became better acquainted with the Latvian or German gentiles with whom they were in regular daily contact, and they soon found out who could be trusted and would be willing to trade food for clothing or jewelry.

During the winter months, many of the people who had been put to work shoveling snow in the streets outside the ghetto, had been taking dangerous chances, running into nearby houses to barter various articles for food, knocking on any door, not knowing who might be behind it. Their risk involved not only being turned over to the authorities or being discovered by their Latvian or German SS taskmasters, but what would happen much more often: the "purchaser" would accept whatever the inmate had to offer and would ostensibly make "payment" with say, flour or butter. But the inmate would later discover to his dismay that his sack of flour contained only spackle underneath a superficial layer of the real thing, or that his slab of butter concealed a heavy rock to make it weigh more. In addition, on the next working day the inmates might be shoveling snow at the other end of town under heavy SS guard, which would make it impossible for them to go to their "customers" of the day before and collect outstanding "debts." This, in turn, frequently led to angry scenes in the ghetto at the end of the day when the inmate who had supplied the clothes or valuables for the barter deal and had expected to get half the food in return, found himself discomfited. Now with the coming of spring, however, the labor details were assigned to work in the same place each day, and such mishaps were rare. Lively trading developed and daring men and women brought badly needed food into the ghetto.

While the inmates had left most of their belongings at the railroad station at the time of their arrival in Riga, the few things they had managed to save always included some items they could do without and could therefore use for barter. In addition, even though they were required to deliver all their valuables to the German authorities, more often then not they had succeeded in retaining something that later could be bartered for food. Although stealing was a very dangerous enterprise, clothes for barter were taken from the *Gewerbebetrieb* as well as from the clothing center; consequently, there was never a let-up in the clandestine trade.

There was still another way—possibly the most dangerous of all—to get goods which could later be bartered. It entailed stealing clothes, such as insulated underwear, socks, and even shoes from the army and air force depots where many ghetto inmates were working. Because the Latvian civilians paid very well for this kind of merchandise, people were willing to risk smuggling clothes into the ghetto in order to have them taken out again by those who had good connections for obtaining food.

Ingenious ways were devised to bring such food into the ghetto. Army-type containers with false bottoms were fashioned, as were regular satchels with hidden pockets, and bags that could be hung under the women's skirts right below the buttocks, thus escaping detection.

Each labor detail had its foreman, an inmate who in most cases saw to it that everyone obtained something. These labor detail foremen, called *Kolonnenfuehrer,* were identified by white armbands bearing their titles. They were usually chosen by chief labor detail administrator Schultz on the day he put the particular labor detail together, or at times, by Commandant Krause himself. On the rare occasions when he chose the workers for various projects, the commandant always selected young, beautiful girls to be in charge of the *Kommando.* In small labor details, the foreman had to work along with the others, but in large details, he or she was usually exempt from work. So as to know when to stop for lunch or when to have the workers prepare to return to the ghetto, each *Kolonnenfuehrer* was allowed to have a wristwatch. Naturally, there was no way to check whether he wore the same watch every day. In this way, many of the watches "illegally" owned by ghetto Jews were smuggled out and exchanged for flour, bacon, butter, or sugar. Food obtained in this manner would be shared on a fifty-fifty basis with the former owner; thus the transaction brought happiness to at least two people.

Very often the labor detail foreman had to report to Schultz or to his assistants on matters concerning the job to which the detail had been assigned. As a gesture of good will,

the detail foremen usually managed to give the ghetto officials some food or cigarettes, and it was considered prudent
to make similar good-will gestures to the ghetto police.

Sometimes, of course, a zealous overseer or an SS guard
would catch an unfortunate in the act of bartering. Even
worse, the contraband might be discovered either by the
commandant or in a body search conducted by an SS man
standing at the entrance as the offender returned to the
ghetto with his labor detail. The ghetto entrance was closed
off by a wooden gate similar to those usually found at railroad crossings. When the columns of laborers returned to the
ghetto from outside work and saw that the gate had been
lowered, they knew immediately that a body search was
taking place and that their "loot" was in danger.

The guards stationed on the outside could often be bribed,
but when the ghetto commandant or his men found evidence
of bartering, it meant death for the offender unless he was
able to talk fast. However, even eloquence did not help when
Krause was in one of his black moods. If the offender was a
man, he would be hanged summarily on Tin Square; if it was
a women, Krause personally took her to the cemetery and
shot her, thus, as the ghetto jargon put it, "getting his satisfaction" for the day.

Although Krause was unpredictable, the general opinion
was that in his depraved mind he craved such an occasional
exercise of his power. Whenever he came back from the cemetery after he had done the job, his face seemed different. It
had lost its usual pinched expression and looked somehow
relaxed.

However, during the summer of 1942, for no apparent
reason, this changed. Krause no longer applied the extreme
penalty when the offender was a woman. Instead, he would
have her hair completely shorn off on the spot by a Jewish
barber. He would then hang a sign around her neck, de-
scribing her "crime" and have her stand in front of the

Kommandantur for the next few hours. All the labor details had to pass by so that they would be sure to see her. The first woman to get off so "cheaply" was Dolly Spiegel of the Prague group. She was exceptionally beautiful, a fact that might have influenced Krause in her favor.

Unfortunately, the ghetto commandant's show of clemency came too late for many who had been found guilty of offenses before the summer. In March, 1942, for instance, Fleischel, the elder of the Hanover group, caught Mary Korwill, who had owned the well-known Tante Mary Children's Camp in Austria, wearing her gold wrist watch. Just as Fleischel was berating her loudly for "illegally" owning jewelry, Krause, in one of his bad moods, happened to come out of the big gate leading onto Berliner Strasse. On learning of Miss Korwill's "crime," he took her directly to the cemetery and shot her. Fleischel and Tante Mary's aged mother were both ordered to watch the execution. The old lady lived on for a long time—until late in the second winter. At times, her mind would wander and she would ask people where her daughter had gone.

Two days before Passover 1942, Krause shot another woman from Vienna, a Mrs. Hauser, who had kept one glove from a pile of woolen wearing apparel that had been set aside as gifts for the soldiers at the front. She had been searched by the SS officer at her place of employment, the Truppenwirtschaftslager of the Waffen SS, and he reported her to the ghetto authorities. Her two teenage daughters, Josephine and Sally, went to the commandant and pleaded for mercy, but he flew into a towering rage and threw them out.[40]

For men, Krause had no pity at all. On Tin Square where the gallows stood, he ordered one of the Latvian SS guards to perform the hangings while he watched intently. If the hanging took place on a Sunday, everyone had to come and watch. In such a case, the victim had to spend his last days until the appointed Sunday inside the ghetto jail, also located on Tin Square. On weekdays, all details returning from work outside, had to pass by the gallows, and if Krause was still there, he admonished them to look. Averting one's eyes was risky business. If Krause noticed it, he would shout at the offender and make him come right up to the swaying corpse.

On one occasion he sentenced a man to death by hanging for having hidden money in his glove. German Jews were not allowed to have any money. This man, Dr. Johann Weiss, a lawyer from Vienna who had been an army officer in World War I, had been brought to the ghetto along with his wife Elizabeth and daughter Hertha. The young girl went to Krause and pleaded for her father's life. When she realized that her pleas were of no avail, she asked the commandant to at least change the sentence from hanging to shooting. Shooting was considered an easier death; hanging, too public and undignified. Krause acceded to her request and shot him. A year after the execution, when Krause had already been transferred and replaced by Eduard Roschmann, the widow and daughter asked permission to visit Weiss's grave. They wanted to comply with the Jewish custom of visiting the grave of their loved one on the anniversary of his death. Roschmann, that most peculiar SS man, permitted them to do so.

In spite of the hangings and shootings, which almost became routine, the people somehow believed that better times were on the horizon. On the meadows behind the houses the grass had begun to sprout, flowers grew on hedges that had seemed so bare and ugly only a short time before, and the vile smells from the cesspools had abated, giving way to the fragrance of lilac bushes in many of the backyards.

The appearance of the ghetto inmates also changed. Heavy coats, shawls, and kerchiefs were relegated to corners and packed away. Shoes, no longer wrapped in rags to keep out the snow and the cold, were cleaned and showed many pretty legs. The mild spring weather made it possible for people to look like respectable human beings again and, with the change in looks, there came a change in attitude. Flushed with newly found strength, they were content to cope with many small annoyances rather than with one big problem. They tackled those daily petty irritations quite successfully, relatively speaking. It was definitely a time for hope, and even more important, a time to devise ways and means for surviving until the hoped-for day of liberation.

6
Education in the Ghetto

As transport after transport arrived in the ghetto and it became clear that each contained many children, Krause had given permission to the Jews to open schools.

In the Vienna group, a large room in one of the buildings of No. 5 Berliner Strasse had been made ready for that purpose, and all children between the ages of four and fourteen were told to go there every day. The teacher in charge was "Tante Mary" Korwill. She was to be shot by Krause only about two months later. In the meantime, though, she was very much alive and determined to give each child the proper training for a better future. Her lesson plans were supervised by Professor Alfred Lemberger who had taught at a gymnasium (academic high school) in Vienna and was now the assistant to Karl Loebl, the elder of the Vienna group in the ghetto. Lemberger was required to work outside the ghetto at least three times a week, and spent the remaining days helping both Loebl and the school.

Tante Mary used a monitorial system through which the older children helped the younger ones. Since there was very little paper, almost no books, and few other paraphernalia usually associated with school, much learning had to be done by rote learning and repetition. Children were taught poems and ballads; they learned entire passages by heart. Thus, the parents had a treat in store for them, for their children could entertain them in the evening by reciting the poems and singing the songs they had learned at Tante Mary's school. Because Tante Mary was an educator with years of experience, the school was quite successful; the children enjoyed

71

going there and made progress in their studies. Tante Mary was strict, but fair. She knew several children who had attended her camp in Austria, but she did not play favorites. Her untimely death was a traumatic experience for the children, who had spent most of their waking hours each day for two whole months under her guidance.

The Berlin group had a rather large school at the corner of Berliner and Leipziger Strasse. The Leipzig group, too, had a large school. Groups having few children, such as the Cologne and Cassel groups, would combine to form one school. There was no lack of trained male teachers, even professors, but the Jewish administrators felt it would be wiser to use mainly female teachers. As it was, the German ghetto had been depleted of its men. Besides, male workers were needed in the city and the inmates knew that the safety of the entire ghetto depended on their willingness to assist in the German war effort.

When the children got home from school, they had other duties awaiting them. The older children would prepare a fire or even cook some food for their hard-working elders who came home later exhausted. Some of the children acted as messengers for the ghetto offices. Several of the older children helped clean the streets and houses. The small children were kept in school until they were picked up, much like in the procedure followed by modern day-care centers; sometimes they were even brought home by their teachers.

The ghetto, a living and breathing community, had its own rhythm. There was an undercurrent of frantic expectation each evening as the sun went down and the labor details were expected to return. The older children, whenever feasible, would be standing near the barbed-wire fence as soon as dusk fell, waiting for their mothers and fathers or even just neighbors to arrive. Sometimes the youngsters were able to warn the returning grown-ups of searches being made for contraband food. In such cases, if the contraband could be eaten as it was, it would be divided among the members of the labor detail who would gobble it up as rapidly as possible. If that was not possible, the precious food would be thrown away in order to avoid punishment. If the Latvian SS guard had turned his back, food could be thrown over the fence to the children waiting on the other side. But that hardly ever happened.

Whenever possible, parents arranged for the distribution of extra food to the teachers because they appreciated what they were doing for their children. This, too, made life in the ghetto seem almost normal at times.

The man in charge of the Berlin group's school was an elderly *Studienrat* (high school teacher). He was permitted to remain inside the ghetto all day because he was too feeble to do any other work. As has already been pointed out, most of the teachers were women and not always well trained; in many cases, therefore, high school teachers with the needed skills and experience would sit down after completing their other work to draw up lesson plans and instruct these teachers as to what they were to teach the next day, just as Professor Lemberger was doing for the Vienna group.

Once the children reached the age of fourteen, their formal education came to an end. They were assigned to labor details and could now regard themselves as grown-ups. Because of "Operation Duenamuende," directed especially against families with small children, the schools prematurely lost many of their students in March 1942. Yet, there were still quite a few children left. These were mostly the sons and daughters of skilled workers who were employed in "safe" labor details and therefore had not been taken away to be liquidated. There were also children of ghetto functionaries who were considered too important to be sent away; among them were the twin sons of labor detail administrator Schultz.[41] In addition, there were children whose parents had escaped the mass killing by going into hiding. Their disobedience to Nazi orders, so uncharacteristic of the docile German Jews, had temporarily saved their own lives and those of their children.

Because of a decrease in the student body, many of the ghetto's schools consolidated. Shortly before Tante Mary's execution, which occurred about ten days after the brutal decimation of the ghetto in "Operation Duenamuende," plans were made to combine the schools of the Prague and Vienna groups. With Tante Mary gone, a young school-teacher, Elizabeth Bergmann, formerly of Bruenn (Brno), Czechoslovakia, took over. Professor Lemberger continued to prepare lesson plans tailored to the needs of each child. He believed that the consolidation of the two schools could bring only benefits: the Viennese children would have a chance to learn some Czech, and the Czech children would learn to speak a better German.

Private lessons were also given. Dr. Schwartz of the Vienna group taught mathematics to older students who went to work during the day and came for lessons on one or two evenings a week. It was customary for his students to bring him gifts, such as an egg that the parents had obtained by barter, or a piece of bread, or whatever else could be spared by a student's family. Dr. Schwartz felt, as did the adults involved, that the continued study of mathematics was very important. It would enable his students to be on a par with their equivalents in the outside world and would be beneficial once they had regained their freedom. The teenagers, of course, did not always agree with this view.

The *Studienrat* who directed the Berlin group's school, gave private lessons in Latin every night. Among his students were several adults. The old gentleman was glad to give instruction free of charge to those who could not pay him, for he loved to hear himself read and lecture. Even though he had lost all his other possessions, he had managed to bring several Latin textbooks into the ghetto—no mean feat for a man of his age. He was thus able both to work and to enjoy himself.

Several times a week, for the modest fee of a thin slice of bread or a bowl of soup, Dr. Weil, formerly a professor of literature at the University of Vienna, gave lectures on Goethe's *Faust.* Each class was devoted to the analysis of several scenes from the play. He forgot the realities of ghetto life to such an extent that he became sarcastic and sometimes even quite angry when a student missed a lecture. Because of his unreasonable attitude, and perhaps also such factors as fatigue and hunger among the listeners, his audience dwindled preceptibly. By the time he reached the second act of *Faust,* only a few students remained to listen to him.

Other lessons, perhaps more relevant to everyday needs, were available, too. Old Mr. Felix taught four of the young boys how to use the carpentry tools that he had found in a shed near No. 3 Berliner Strasse. He had been the owner of a furniture store before the war, but had started out as a master carpenter. He was glad to teach the boys whatever he could. His endeavors were crowned with success, for when labor detail administrator Schultz needed carpenters in that late summer, two of Felix's apprentices volunteered and were added to a prestigious labor detail. Both became veritable specialists and got the privilege of extra food rations. When it came to special favors, they did not forget their mentor.

Returnees from Salaspils, once they had recovered from their ordeal, were added to labor details where they could learn trades either from Latvian Jews or German foremen. This was done quite deliberately by the Jewish authorities who knew these young men could be trained rather quickly. Thus, trainees soon became skilled plumbers, painters, electricians, roofers, auto-mechanics, and welders, occupations which later were to save their lives.

Young women, too, learned certain trades, although their training was not as specialized as that given to the men. There were some firms and factories that did not discriminate on the basis of sex. The famous Riga *Gummifabrik,* a factory producing galoshes and boots for soldiers, actually preferred young women. This plant had an excellent training program and eventually employed 200 Jewish girls in what was called a "closed" or "safe" Kommando. It was not possible to request a transfer from this labor detail, but then no one could be removed from it, either.

Seamstresses were needed, too. Many of the older women knew how to sew, albeit not in professional way, but they improved their skills and soon became experts. At the same time, they showed the younger women and girls how to use the sewing machines and to make buttonholes. Through such training methods, the number of skilled workers in the ghetto showed a decided increase. Thus, the Jews, ever ready to accommodate and adapt themselves, kept on learning. It did not matter whether their studies were academic or vocational. What mattered was that they improved their prospects for survival.

7

Zionist and Cultural Activities

Once ghetto life had returned to relative normalcy after "Operation Duenamuende" in March, 1942, the teenagers of the two ghettos in Riga began to discover one another. The Latvian Jewish police, most of whom were members of Betar, a right-wing revisionist Zionist group,* found members of the same organization among the young people from Germany, Austria, and Czechoslovakia. They soon arranged for Friday night meetings, where Betar songs and speeches were the order of the day. Their positions in the police force gave these young men considerable freedom of movement. They were on good terms with the German Jewish police and with their help had set aside a large room in a house near the hospital, where most of these meetings were held. They would casually saunter along Leipziger Strasse to check whether anyone was there, and, if the coast was clear, they could safely cross the border between the Latvian and German ghettos and slip into the house on the German side.

The Latvian Jewish police approved heartily of the schools that had been set up in the German ghetto and at one point even proposed that modern Hebrew be taught to all the children. This idea was not followed up. Nevertheless, the Friday night meetings were very successful and were attended by young people of other Zionist organizations as well, once word of the meetings had gotten around. At that time,

---

*The revisionists formed a militant party within the Zionist movement that, from its inception, openly and actively opposed the anti-Jewish policies of the British authorities in Palestine prior to the establishment of the state of Israel.

differences in ideology seemed irrelevant. What was important to those who came were the Hebrew songs and the spirit of the young people from the two ghettos, who all hoped to go to Palestine some day. Even the pessimists among them declared in their speeches that their only hope after all the indignities and tragedies they had experienced, was emigration to Palestine once the war was over.

Some of the older people came to these gatherings too. Often, there was standing room only as the candles were lit by one of the girls, and the *Oneg Shabbat,* the Friday night celebration of the Sabbath, began. Sometimes, when the older people would cry, the younger ones became impatient with them, and would dance the Hora with abandon until late at night, long after the curfew. At last, one by one, silently and carefully, they would finally make their way home. The Latvian Jewish police were always the last to leave, so as to be able to intervene in case of trouble.

Because of the curfew, those attending these evening affairs ran the risk of being caught either by an unsympathetic German Jewish policeman, whom even these boys could not cajole into forgetting his duty, or by the Jewish group inspectors, of whom some took their jobs quite seriously. The offenders then would receive the punishment of being made to clean the hated cesspools. But the greatest danger, especially during those early months, came from the Latvian SS guards who patrolled the area immediately beyond the ghetto. It was they who were in charge during these hours, for in the evening the German SS usually left the ghetto. The Latvian guards would shoot at anything that moved during the curfew hours. They frequently entered the ghetto, broke into apartments and took away whatever they fancied. There were also numerous cases of rape. People began to barricade their apartments before going to sleep; however, this posed something of a problem because most of the toilets were situated not in the apartments but in the hallways.

Finally, one night early in May, 1942, Commandant Krause, who had been told about these incursions, took it into his head to make a random inspection of apartments on Berliner Strasse during the night. It seems that trouble had been reported the night before. His choice fell on No. 13, on the Viennese side of the street. Escorted by German SS men as well as Jewish ghetto police, he tried to enter an apartment on the second floor, which was shared by several women, including Mrs. Rosa Maier. Since she could not believe that it was indeed Commandant Krause, she refused to open the barricaded door and told him in no uncertain terms where he could go. Only after the intervention of Mager, one of the Viennese policemen, did she finally open the door and, arms akimbo, look up at the scowling SS men and their leader. The language she had used was a rather low Viennese dialect, and Krause, a native of Breslau, understood only half of what she had said. Nevertheless, he got the gist of it. But because he happened to be in one of his kindlier moods just then, he merely laughed and promised her that she would never have to be afraid again. After this incident, the Latvian guards stopped making nightly forays into the ghetto. Three of the original twenty-six Latvian guards were never seen again. Rumor had it that they had been sent to the front. Their fate did not concern us, but Mrs. Maier was regarded as a type of "mascot" for her house from then on.

Following "Operation Duenamuende," the Berlin, Hannover, and Vienna groups had been consolidated under one elder, Guenther Fleischel of Hanover. However, each group kept its own female administrator in charge of labor details. These three women shared an office at No. 4 Berliner Strasse; Fleischel had his office upstairs, complete with two pretty secretaries, Putti Israel and Mady Kreutzer. He did not really like to sit behind his huge desk but preferred to be on the move, constantly alert to whatever was happening in the ghetto. He was not liked or trusted by the inmates. He was respected grudgingly, but people were afraid of him. As for the other group elders, they did not like him at all, because Krause, the commandant, always held him up as an example. Some might have disliked him simply because he was a Catholic, but even those inmates who attended the Catholic services that he conducted at his apartment considered him strange and avoided him except at "church time." He had an explosive temper and, unlike the other ghetto functionaries, he sometimes slapped inmates found guilty of minor offenses.

Both Fleischel and Sonnenschein, the inspector of the Vienna group, kept a careful watch on the house at No. 5 Berliner Strasse, where the school was located. Neither man liked the idea that the room which served as a school during the day was used on Saturday and Sunday nights for social gatherings of teenagers. Dances were held there every week. Some of the young men had managed to hold on to their musical instruments. Walter Turteltaub, a hunchback, was the proud owner of a guitar; Alfred Schatten had a banjo; and Fritz Brunn and Erich Pinkassowitsch each had harmonicas. They were always willing to provide the music for the weekend "socials." One enterprising young fellow, Ludwig Pick of the Prague group, had discovered a record player at his workplace outside the ghetto. He had skillfully taken it apart and brought it virtually piecemeal into the ghetto to avoid being discovered. Once safely inside the ghetto, he reassembled the record player and it remained in use until September, 1943.

Other enterprising youngsters stole phonograph records from their places of employment; in this manner teenagers were able to keep abreast of the latest German hit songs. In other groups, the process was essentially the same. In the Leipzig group, dances were held at the home of the Simmons family, whose son had smuggled in a fabulous collection of records.

Fleischel knew what was going on, and he did not like it.

He might have been genuinely worried about trouble from Krause, and therefore often threatened to close the place down, but he never carried out his threat.

Starting in May, every Sunday afternoon the people congregated on some of the vacant lots behind their houses. They enjoyed not only the newly sprouted grass and the fresh air, but also the concerts, that had begun spontaneously one day and continued thereafter. A very talented young woman, Grete Picker, was always ready to sing; others, not so talented but equally willing, would sing or tell jokes, and get applause. The star, however, was always Miss Picker. People from all the other groups came to the open space formed by the courtyards of Nos. 5, 7, and 9 Berliner Strasse, and those of Nos. 25, 27, and 29 Moskauer Strasse. Listening to the music and looking at the profusion of lilac bushes in bloom, one could almost forget that one was a prisoner. But reminders were never far away.

A few times during that summer of 1942, Commandant Krause, flanked by his chauffeur Max Gymnich and *Oberwachtmeister** Neumann, would come to listen to the singing. They did not sit down on the grass with the others but leaned against one of the buildings or against a tree and smoked cigarettes. When the people rose, Krause motioned for them to sit down again. Once the commandant brought with him a surprise guest, a man whom the inmates still remembered well. He was Anton Brunner, the Gestapo official who had been in charge of deportations from Vienna. Now here he was, Anton Brunner, standing in the middle of the Riga Ghetto, listening to the lilting Viennese tunes and merrily humming along. It was obvious that he was having a good time, and he was not the only one, for the music made people forget how dismal their lives really were.

---

*Squad sergeant major

Of the more than 5,000 Jews whom Brunner had sent to Riga, only about 900 were then still alive. It was clear that almost everyone present recognized him, and he seemed to enjoy his notoriety. The procedure governing the mass deportations of Jews from Vienna involved rounding up Jews from all over the city and putting them into empty public school buildings. There Anton Brunner decided who would be sent "east" and who would be permitted to remain in Vienna for the time being. He was a short man, of sadistic bent, who obviously relished his power. At night he would go down to the "bunker," the school basement that was used as a temporary jail to harass the Jewish "security risks" who had been picked up for such offenses as being seen in the street without wearing the yellow Star of David or attempting to shop at a store at the wrong time of day. Another one of his delights was to surprise the women prisoners in the school washroom.

At his trial in Vienna in 1946, Brunner denied that he had ever been to Riga. He insisted that he had not known where the Jews had been sent from Vienna and could therefore not be held responsible for anything that had happened to them. But several survivors who had seen him in Riga with Krause that lovely day in May and had heard him humming along with the others, were able to identify him. He was convicted and hanged.[42]

At one of the Sunday afternoon concerts in the Riga Ghetto, Krause spotted Mrs. Maier, the woman from Vienna who had given him a piece of her mind a few months before. He made her come forward and sing. Mrs. Maier, ever resourceful, chose a Viennese dialect drinking song, all about wine, women, and song. She did quite well, got thunderous applause, and Krause fairly beamed.

More formal concerts were held on several occasions under the auspices of the Cologne and Cassel groups. The Viennese sent Erich Eichenbaum, a concert violinist, who had managed to keep his precious Italian violin. His concerts gave much pleasure to others and also to himself. His wife, Gertrude, maintained that only the violin could make him forget that he was hungry and that he was a prisoner under conditions especially unbearable for a sensitive artist.

The Latvian Jews were represented by another concert violinist, Brandt, who also owned an excellent violin. A good cello was supplied by none other than Krause; it had been found in luggage left at the station and the commandant appropriated it for the orchestra. But the problem was where to find someone to play it, for the original owner of the cello, a Jew from Dortmund whose name no one knew, had been laid to rest long before in the mass grave at Salaspils. Krause brought in other instruments as well, and the orchestra gave several performances. Their programs consisted of Brahms, Haydn, Mozart, and Beethoven, and the hush which settled over the audience was the same that falls over concert audiences all over the free world when the music begins.

For cultural affairs such as these the Latvian Jewish performers had to obtain passes to be able to cross into the German ghetto and back to their own ghetto again. No cultural event was ever held in the Latvian ghetto where the atmosphere was entirely different from that of its German counterpart. Perhaps the total absence of women in the Latvian ghetto had something to do with it.

The German ghetto not only had concerts but also dramatic performances. Krause, who was quite enthusiastic about the idea, became an eager patron of the ghetto theater.

In order to insure large audiences, the concerts and plays were performed in the largest "auditorium" available, namely, in the same factory-type building where the ghetto inmates were put to work sorting the clothes left behind by the dead. Each play had a run of several weeks, with performances given on Saturday and Sunday nights. Seating was on a "first come, first sit" basis, although some reserved tickets were available at the offices of the various groups. The three front rows of chairs were saved for the ghetto elite and for those with reserved seats. The other rows consisted of long benches. A stage and a beautiful curtain gave the large hall, temporarily cleared of the bundles that recalled mass murder, the respectable look of a theater. The plays presented were mainly the old classics, such as Lessing's *Nathan the Wise,* Zweig's *Jeremias,* the first act of Goethe's *Faust,* and *Everyman,* the play made famous by Max Reinhardt. On several occasions the groups cooperated in staging variety shows, making use of talented singers and comedians among the inmates. A good band was formed, too, which included a number of young Latvian Jews and played mainly American hits of the 1930s. This group even composed a march for the ghetto police.

Although it was relatively easy for Latvian Jews to get passes to enter the German ghetto for cultural events, few of them ever attempted to go to the German ghetto for the performances given by their compatriots. There were several reasons for their indifference. Primarily, they felt that the efforts of the German Jews to lead a relatively normal life in the ghetto were a mockery. Those few Latvian Jews who participated in the cultural programs of the German, Austrian, and Czech Jews frequently found themselves targets of ridicule in their group, but the desire to escape their drab, hopeless existence, if only for a few short hours, must have been stronger than the fear of contempt and criticism from their countrymen.

Krause went to the concerts and never missed the "opening night" of a stage production. He always came with an entourage of other German officials, some of whom the inmates did not know. On these occasions, the barriers between Nazis and Jews, between murderers and victims, seemed to disappear. Krause and the other Germans sat in the first row, surrounded by the Jews with whom they were in daily contact, enjoying and applauding the various programs.

The inmates of the ghetto looked forward eagerly to each performance, and these events were very much appreciated. It is hard to tell whether anyone—performer or spectator— ever consciously thought of his personal involvement as a form of resistance. Those who put on the shows or organized the concerts may have done so to bring some color into the drabness of ghetto existence and to demonstrate that the desire for the finer things of life was stronger than barbed-wire fences. Theirs may have been a deep need to elevate others from the level of mere existence. Their only payment was applause; yet, throughout the two years that the ghetto lasted, they felt compelled to go on. The obvious delight with which the German authorities greeted these events may have been a factor as well. Artists and audience alike were flattered by the presence of the commandant and his entourage in their midst. They regarded it as a compliment to the talents of the performers.

Hindsight permits us to admire these efforts and to recognize them as the expressions of an indomitable spirit. But at the time they seemed merely a natural reflection of the prisoners' former life style.

Many ghetto songs were composed and quickly became popular. They were mainly based on well-known tunes, and they dealt with ghetto romances between Jewish boys from Latvia and Jewish girls from Germany, or with more practical matters such as bartering in Skirotava. A more somber note was struck by the song which many regarded as the anthem of the ghetto. It was based on a famous prison song, "Die Moorsoldaten" (The Peat Bog Soldiers), and it ended with the lament that people should have been banished to a far-off, sinister place for no other reason but that they were Jews.

8
Romance in the Ghetto

It was common knowledge in the ghetto that Commandant Kurt Krause was quite fond of one Jewess, the beautiful Olly Adler who had been sent to Riga from Vienna in January and had been made a member of the Prague group. Krause permitted her to run the ghetto's only beauty parlor on Prager Strasse, complete with hair dryers, mirrors, and wash basins. He also saw to it that her younger sister, Gerda Hacker, was assigned to a labor detail which was known to be very desirable because those employed in it had lots of chances to get food.

In addition to the commandant, any SS man in the ghetto who wanted to help a Jew, or more often a Jewess, could easily get him or her into a "good" labor detail by just contacting Schultz, the labor detail administrator. Krause seldom interfered with labor detail assignments, but whenever he liked a young girl, he would see to it that she got a better job. He was reported to have also had several affairs with other Jewish girls in the ghetto besides Olly Adler. Consorting with a Jewess was a serious crime; it was referred to as *Rassenschande* (racial violation); and the usual punishment was death for the Jew and either prison or death for the "Aryan" partner. But Krause did not seem to fear the consequences. The Riga Ghetto seemed oblivious to any laws except those made by Krause, and apparently the stigma of Rassenschande did not bother him, nor was he the only German to feel that way. Oberwachtmeister Neumann had a girl friend from the Leipzig group, whom he met regularly in the garden in back of No. 17 Berliner Strasse. Krause's chauffeur,

87

Gymnich, was very friendly with a girl from the Cologne group, and rumor had it that he even smuggled letters from her to Gentile friends in the Reich.

Since there was not too much to do at the beauty parlor, it became a hangout for the ghetto's elite, who would stop in and chat with Olly. Yet, though she enjoyed a certain status, most of the ghetto inmates regarded her not as another Queen Esther, but simply as a Jewish girl who had compromised herself.

Olly's beauty proved to be her undoing. After the liquidation of the ghetto, Olly, along with all the others, was taken to Camp Kaiserwald. There, Hannes, one of the Gentile "professional criminals" imprisoned at the camp, fell in love with her. The affair was quite obvious, and Emilie Kowa, the SS overseer of women, reported it. It was believed that Kowa herself liked Hannes and therefore wanted to be rid of her hated rival. Olly was shot at the Central Prison, but Hannes was merely transferred to one of the camps in the vicinity. When he later returned to Kaiserwald, rumor had it that he had now transferred his affections to Emilie Kowa, since he once remarked that he had exchanged "a goose for a swan."[43]

But all that still lay in the future. In the spring of 1942, Olly could be seen walking around on her high heels, enjoying the change in the weather along with everyone else. After a few false starts and unexpected snow flurries late in April, life for the ghetto population became easier. In back of most of the houses, people created small vegetable gardens. Some of these gardens were surprisingly beautiful and served as proper backdrops for the young couples who braved the curfew and probably told each other the same things that boys and girls in love have told each other since the beginning of time.

Sometimes the gardeners, usually the house commanders, got quite ambitious. Mr. Felix, the man in charge of No. 3

Berliner Strasse, even grew watermelons. The largest garden was the one behind the hospital. It had a hothouse, for which the glass had been brought in by order of Commandant Krause. Several older people who had, or said they had, experience with raising vegetables, were employed there. While the produce was mainly intended for the German authorities, the inmates of the ghetto were able to obtain vegetables for themselves also, especially if they knew one of the gardeners.

The vegetables that were grown in the ghetto were a sorely needed addition to existing rations, which had not been increased in months. Each person still received 220 grams of bread per day, one portion of somewhat tainted fish per week, an occasional serving of turnips, sour cabbage, or frozen potatoes, and from time to time, one portion of horse meat. The few small children who were still around, received one liter of fat-free milk per week.[44]

The warm weather was not the only thing that revived people's hopes; good news was coming in from the world outside. Inmates who worked in the city cleaning the apartments of high-ranking SS officials risked their lives to listen to BBC broadcasts. They brought back the news that the United States, Britain, the Soviet Union, and China had joined forces and planned to combine their resources against the common enemy. The people of the ghetto believed that Germany would not be able to hold out long against such a solid show of strength. Whenever people visited each other, the talk turned to politics and the promise of the future. The reliable sources for news from the BBC were Elvira Altschul, Margit Reckler, and Wilma Gerstman. All three were always alone in the apartments that they had to clean and regularly listened to the news broadcasts from England. Of the three, only Mrs. Altschul survived the war.

Ghetto inmates who went out to work in cleaning details and hospital kitchens in the city, saw German soldiers being brought back from the Russian front, sometimes completely demoralized, with frozen toes and fingers. Jokes comparing Hitler to Napoleon made the rounds of the ghetto. Both these two would-be masters of the world had tried to take on the Russian winter; Napoleon had failed, and Hitler would certainly follow him in ignominious defeat. Added to these hopes was the conviction that those who had survived in the ghetto thus far would remain alive because the Germans were badly in need of their services as workers for the war effort.

The stirrings of hope moved not only in the mind but also assumed physical expressions. Before long, the German authorities, evidently noticing an increase in abortions, circulated an order that sexual relations between ghetto inmates would henceforth be forbidden. They did not want the labor force diminished even for the few days needed by a woman to recuperate from the operation. Posters to the effect that sex was *verboten* were placed on the doors of the houses. At no time, however, was any serious attempt made to enforce this new regulation, simply because there was really no way of doing so as long as families lived together.

During that summer of 1942, the group doctors gave all of the teenagers lectures on venereal diseases and contraception. Dr. Rolf Bischofswerder, a young physician from Cologne who now practiced in the Vienna group, was quite frank about the matter. He warned the young women not to become pregnant, telling them that they might well suffer the penalty of sterilization, and this, in his words, would be "a tragedy for you, once this war is over and we are all free again."

Unfortunately, Dr. Bischofswerder did not live to become free again himself. In September, 1944, he and his wife Ruth escaped from Camp Kaiserwald, believing that liberation was at hand. While this was indeed true—the Russians were to take Riga on October 14—these two fugitives, together with their accomplice, Lotte Adler of Cologne, were found by the Germans, brought back to the camp, and executed.

Back in 1942, though, another reason for renewed hope in the ghetto was the fact that Camp Salaspils was slowly being emptied of Jews and, starting in June, each week brought badly undernourished skeletal men back from the camp to the ghetto. It was a happy homecoming, and the inmates of the ghetto made an all-out effort to restore the strength of those who came back. Labor details, returning to the ghetto at the end of each day, were asked to contribute a little of their contraband for the Salaspils returnees. Everyone gave willingly, and within a relatively short time, some of them recuperated, much to the joy of their families, except perhaps in those few cases where the husband or boy friend returning from Salaspils found his place taken by another man, most likely a Latvian Jew.

Among those who came back to the ghetto was a Czech Jew known as "the hangman of Salaspils." Before the war, back in Czechoslovakia, he had been a prizefighter. Now, the survivors of Salaspils had tales to tell of how quick and adept he had been at performing his grisly task so as not to prolong the agony of his victims. Clearly, he had had no other choice but to do the job assigned to him, if he was to save his own life. Only those who had never been put to the test themselves could find it in their hearts to condemn him. In fact, some of the ghetto inmates even liked him, because he was a simple, friendly sort. Once back in the ghetto, he was assigned to the police force and resumed a normal life. He entered into a "ghetto marriage" with Mrs. Rosa Maier (the lady from Vienna who had talked back to Krause) whom he had met on one of his trips to the ghetto. They lived together until they were sent to Camp Kaiserwald, where they were separated. Neither of them survived the war.

The law against sexual relationships, which at first had given rise to all sorts of jokes, eventually led to what young Dr. Bischofswerder and his colleagues had feared all along. On Krause's order, sterilizations were to be performed on all women coming in for second abortions. It was a sinister order, even though compliance with it was rather sketchy, inasmuch as there was never an SS physician at the hospital. Sterilization was performed only when a woman asked for it or when her condition warranted it, as in the event of some female disorders. In such cases a hysterectomy was performed in order to forestall future trouble.

While an abortion was jokingly referred to as "an appendicitis with arms and legs," it was no laughing matter for the men and women directly involved. Even though Krause could not really tell whether the woman had been sterilized, he could and did order from ten to twenty-five lashes for the man, to be administered either at the hospital or at the ghetto police station. If, as happened more than once, a girl refused to give the name of her partner, she was punished by having to go through the operation without anesthesia. It was to avoid both the corporal punishment of the men and the suffering of the women that the secret hospital room had been set up in the Cassel sector of the ghetto, but it was far too small to accommodate everyone.

Eduard Roschmann, who succeeded Krause as commandant of the ghetto, preferred not to be the sole arbiter of laws as his predecessor had been. He sent the man involved to the Central Prison, from which he might or might not come back, depending on the treatment meted out to him, and on his stamina. As far as the girl was concerned, Roschmann simply ordered that she should get no anesthesia and then he left the scene, since he had no stomach to watch the proceedings. Thus, the doctors were able to ignore his orders.

Other operations were performed as well. In most cases, people recovered and went back to work after their convalescence. There was a high incidence of boils which had to be lanced and other infections too. There were broken bones to be set. Many men suffered from hernias which resulted from lifting heavy objects. In short, the ghetto hospital was always busy.

In spite of the stringent laws about sex, "ghetto marriages" were still made and most certainly consummated. Isser Lurie, a Latvian Jew who was a jewelry designer and engraver, fashioned the rings used by these happy couples. The rings were made of silver, sometimes with a thin golden plating or edge, and always with the initials of the couple and the date. Eventually, the rings were not only used as wedding bands, but became a popular fashion item as well. At his place of work—a clothing depot for the German air force—Lurie even received orders from German soldiers to make up rings for them, too. His business was lucrative, and his prices were steep; he lowered his prices only for bona fide ghetto couples, for this small, gentle craftsman believed in making people happy.[4] [5]

There was little difficulty if both partners in the "marriage" were from the same group, because they lived in the same sector of the ghetto. The couple would simply take up residence together, the woman would change her last name— usually, she would combine it with that of the man—and that was all. But when it came to liaisons between partners not belonging to the same group, the ghetto bureaucracy was not so complaisant because their statistical bookkeeping became more complicated. How could they account in their daily reports for individuals moving from one sector to another when marriages and sexual relationships were forbidden? Therefore, in such cases, each partner officially remained within his or her group, even if in fact, the couple now shared the same quarters. The SS never knew what went on; and even if they did, it is doubtful that they would have cared whether or not individuals changed groups. Still, one had to be careful. For this reason, some people considered themselves married without informing even the Jewish authorities; they probably felt that it was best to remain as inconspicuous as possible.

Worst of all, from the standpoint of the ghetto

bureaucracy, were partnerships involving a man from the Latvian ghetto and a woman from the German ghetto. Despite the obvious cultural differences, such romances were rather common occurrences, given the fact that almost all the women in the Latvian ghetto had been killed off, while much of the male population of the German ghetto had gone to Salaspils. However, the Latvian and German ghettos were not only two distinct administrative units but were also separated by physical barriers. As a result, Latvian Jewish men could not move into the German ghetto, nor could German Jewish women move into the Latvian ghetto. As a matter of fact, although men from the Latvian ghetto could get passes to visit the German ghetto, women from the German ghetto were never permitted in the Latvian ghetto at all, not even for visits. Thus, marriage between such partners, even in the ghetto sense of the term, was impossible. Nevertheless, quite a few permanent arrangements existed between inmates of the two ghettos. The couples lived apart all week and saw each other on Sundays. It took skill on their part and much good will on the part of neighbors to give the couples some privacy. But love conquers all, and, where the partners managed to survive the war, many of these "ghetto marriages" have endured to this day.

9
Resistance

The spiritual and cultural leaders of the German ghetto—not necessarily the administrative functionaries—but people like Dr. Schwartz (the mathematics teacher of the Vienna group), Professor Lemberger (who planned the lessons for the Vienna group school), Elizabeth Bergmann (Tante Mary's successor), and Dr. Bischofswerder of the Cologne group—never ceased to impress upon the young people that the first law of resistance was survival. The day-to-day struggle to cope with ghetto conditions required live people, not dead heroes.

Most of the young people in the ghetto took these admonitions seriously and conducted themselves accordingly, but there were a few outstanding instances of death-defying courage.

In January, 1942, two young boys had escaped from Camp Salaspils. *Obersturmbannfuehrer* Rudolf Lange, escorted by his deputy Maywald and other SS men, ordered Horst Wertheim, the elder of Barrack 2 at the camp, to select ten men as hostages, who were to die in atonement for the boys' escape. Wertheim, who was twenty-two, stiffened. In a clear voice, audible to the more than 1,000 emaciated men standing at attention, he said to Lange: "Sir, let me be the first hostage. The other nine you will have to pick out yourself!"

It was apparent that this courageous reply came as a surprise to Lange and his cohorts; they had not encountered this kind of behavior before. The Jews, in the eyes of the SS, were not only enemies of the German people; they were destroyers of German culture, they were saboteurs, and, last but not least, they were portrayed as cowards. Here, however, was a man who had chosen to die rather than cooperate with his murderers.

Other incidents of defiance, in the form of curses or other invective hurled at the Nazi overlords, occurred mainly at the cemetery or underneath the gallows, when the condemned felt he had nothing more to lose. The victims were quickly silenced by the brutal fists of the guards. But the surviving inmates of the ghetto cherished these last words of their comrades, knowing well that the doomed men had suffered vicious beatings before being finally put to death, but had felt they had to leave a message before they died.

On the same day that ghetto Commandant Krause gave permission for the baking of Passover matzoth, he sentenced two young Latvian Jews to death for having been caught with cigarettes. He was apparently in a good mood that day, for he decided to shoot the two offenders rather than give them the usual punishment of hanging. One of the young men asked to be allowed to smoke one last cigarette before dying, and Krause, still in an expansive frame of mind, acceded to his request.

As the cigarette got smaller, the young Latvian Jew pointed to the ashes, flicked them off, and said to Krause: "You see, one day Germany will crumble, just like these ashes!" Enraged, Krause slapped him and then shot him. This and similar incidents were later reported by Guenther Fleischel or other elders or by some of the Jewish policemen standing guard at the cemetery.

Most of the German Jews, preoccupied with their own survival and that of their immediate families, paid only fleeting attention to these daily tragedies. But the Latvian Jews seemed more affected. They were able to visit the German ghetto quite easily now. First it was the musicians, and now the soccer teams, especially that of the Latvian Jewish police, which played against the Jewish police of the German ghetto. The games were held on the same Tin Square where the gallows stood.

The star of the matches was the Latvians' goalie, Schulmann. A prizefighter before the war, Schulmann had superb reflexes. Even the SS was impressed. They came whenever there was a match and their presence did not dampen the general excitement. They and everybody else, especially the girls, rooted for Schulmann.

Thus, each and every Sunday, the Latvian Jews armed with passes, came to the German ghetto, ready to enjoy themselves, but on the alert all the time. Actually, they visited the German ghetto on other occasions as well. On most Friday nights, Oneg Shabbats were still held and the discussions sometimes took militant turns. The young Jewish policemen, the elite of the Latvian ghetto, spoke about the need for armed resistance. Unknown to them, similar thoughts were being voiced in other ghettos as well, but since there was no contact among the various ghettos, it may be assumed that individual ghetto uprisings were spontaneous acts rather than part of a widespread, organized effort.

Accordingly, plans for an uprising were made in the Riga Ghetto, but only a few of the police were in on the plans. When several dissident Latvian Jews left the ghetto by truck to join the partisans instead of remaining and taking part in an eventual uprising, they ran into an ambush and managed to kill several Germans. The result was a surprise search conducted by the Germans within the Latvian ghetto. The Nazis discovered an arsenal of guns and even a small, obsolete cannon in a bunker, the entrance to which was through an oven. The weapons had been smuggled in piece by piece by a labor detail employed at the Pulverturm, a storage depot for weapons and ammunition. The searchers also found a list of people involved in the plot and several maps of strategic points to be attacked.

Immediately, the forty-one members of the Latvian Jewish

police were arrested and put under heavy SS guard in the Kommandantur on Leipziger Strasse. Actually, only a few of them were implicated by the list of names found in the bunker, but the German authorities apparently assumed that all of them would be sympathetic to an uprising. They were young, they were strong and healthy, and most of them no longer had families; thus, they might well feel that they had nothing to lose. It is true, however, that most of them had girl friends in the German ghetto, but it could be assumed that under the circumstances their desire for revenge would be stronger than any wish they might have for new love relationships at that time. Also, the German authorities knew that the Latvian Jews were much more pessimistic about their chances for survival than the inmates of the German ghetto. Based on their evaluation of the facts, the Germans concluded that the Latvian Jews would be willing to chance death more readily than their fellow Jews from Germany, Austria, and Czechoslovakia. Even if they had taken no active part in planning the uprising, the authorities believed that, as members of the ghetto police force, they had certainly been aware of the plans and were thus at least indirectly involved.

On Friday night, October 29, 1942, all the inmates of the ghetto, both German and Latvian, were ordered to report to their assembly points a quarter of an hour earlier that next morning. On Saturday, October 30, both ghettos swarmed with SS men. Present in the courtyard of the Kommandantur, in addition to the commandant, were *Obersturmbannfuehrer* Lange, the head of *Einsatzkommando 2C,* his deputy, Maywald, Nickel and Migge, commandant and deputy commandant, respectively, of Salaspils, and several of the usual ghetto personnel. All forty-one members of the Latvian Jewish police were brought to the courtyard as well.

Meanwhile, at the exit of the Latvian ghetto, about 300 older men were put onto waiting trucks and taken away. It was said that their names had been on the lists found in the search, but they were merely counted and not called by name. Both the elder of the Latvian ghetto and the man in charge of labor details were arrested and brought to the ghetto jail. After that was over, all the other inmates were permitted to proceed to their places of work as usual, but the forty-one "suspects" still remained standing in the courtyard.

At about 10:30 A.M., the entire Latvian Jewish police force was taken through the big gate of the so-called Saxony House and was marched to Tin Square, followed by a contingent of SS men. The doomed Jews knew what was coming. Upon a signal from one of them, they tried to disperse. Immediately, the machine guns opened fire and forty of the forty-one were killed. The one survivor who managed to escape stumbled into the cellar at the Cassel Court, where potatoes were being sorted, and asked the workers to hide him. They threw old bags over him, but the SS soon found him, dragged him out, and shot him, too.[46] This was the end of the police force of the Latvian ghetto.

In the general confusion, one SS man, too, was shot and killed. His comrades put up a small sign at the edge of Tin Square to commemorate the place where he fell.

The blood-soaked soil where the Jewish policemen died was later scooped up by several of the murdered men's girl friends, who placed the soil into little bags which they tied around their necks.

A rumor soon spread through the Latvian ghetto that the forty-one victims had been turned in by none other than Rudolf Haar, the chief of the German Jewish ghetto police, who allegedly had overheard them discussing their plans for an armed uprising. It was said in Haar's defense that he had feared for the safety of the entire ghetto, both German and Latvian, if the young men had been allowed to carry out their plan. However, this rumor was not founded on fact: Haar had not informed on his Latvian fellow Jews. Only afterwards, when Lange and Krause had threatened to liquidate the German as well as the Latvian ghetto, had Haar gone to the two Nazis and told them that the German Jews had had no part in the uprising and should therefore not be punished. But it was Haar's long-standing and well-known dislike for the *Ostjuden* that rendered him suspect in the eyes of the Latvian ghetto. There was still another reason: if Krause had not been accompanied by members of the German Jewish police during the search for the secret arsenal, no one would have thought of implicating Haar. But the fact that men under Haar's command had been members of the search team along with the Nazis, made Haar look so guilty that, in their anger, the inmates of the Latvian ghetto overlooked one basic fact: the location of the secret arms depot had been given away to the SS by one of their own men, a Latvian Jew, who had been on the ambushed truck and had broken down under torture.

After the liquidation of the ghetto, Haar was brought to Camp Kaiserwald. On the second or third night after his arrival, he was pushed into the cesspool, head first, pulled out and pushed in over and over again, until he died. As he was being dragged to the cesspool, he kept screaming that he had not betrayed anyone. According to the camp's grapevine, Haar's execution had been arranged by the bereaved girl friends of the murdered Latvian Jews. The actual job, however, had not been done by Jews but by Gentiles who had been interned at Kaiserwald as "professional criminals." The commandant of Kaiserwald had the incident investigated, but the culprits were never found.

Thus the summer of 1942 came to a dreadful end. The earlier complacency was gone and with it, some of the hope. The prospect of another winter in the ghetto loomed threateningly, and the people sorely missed the handsome young men whom they had passed each day on their way to and from the ghetto with their labor details. They had always been helpful, offering a kind word to everyone, and so their absence was a painful void in the lives of the surviving ghetto inmates. Besides, the memory of what had happened to these members of the ghetto police, was a constant reminder that the same thing could also happen to all the Jews of the ghetto at any time.

10
The Second Winter

After a brief autumn, which had transformed the drab ghetto into a burst of colors, the people settled down to face yet another winter of imprisonment. But this time, it seemed in some ways to be an easier winter than the one before. This was due in part to existing sanitary regulations and to the fact that the water pipes inside the houses kept on working, and also to the sad truth that—alas—the ghetto was not so crowded any longer.

The one great enemy was still the bitter cold; firewood was very scarce. Under their watchful eyes, the SS permitted forays into the empty houses around the ghetto so that any remaining furniture could be brought back to the ghetto and used for firewood. These were the houses that had never been turned over to the German Jews after the massacre of the Latvian Jews, but had been left empty so as to form a *cordon sanitaire* between the ghetto and the outside world.

The wood was too precious to be used exclusively for heating. Instead, it was used mainly for cooking, even though food was in rather short supply just then. The culinary creativity of the women reached new heights. What they could do with the ghetto fare, only slightly augmented by contraband, bordered on the miraculous.

The Day of Atonement had come and gone, and the prayers for deliverance had remained unanswered. Those who fasted on that holiest of days did not find it too difficult to go without food for twenty-four hours; by now they were used to never having a full stomach. The German authorities had taken no notice of the Jewish religious calendar. In general,

103

they paid little attention to the inmates, a fact which, in spite of physical discomforts, lulled many into a false sense of security.

News began to filter into the ghetto that the war was not going well for the Germans. Reports of the battle of Stalingrad came from inmates who had contacts with the world outside other than through bartering. These contacts were seldom with the SS, but mostly with regular German army, navy, or air force personnel, many of whom did not condone the brutal methods of the SS and treated the Jews working for them like human beings. Other good news from the battlefront was brought by thousands of Russian prisoners of war who were stationed in and around Riga and had managed to make contact with labor details from the ghetto.

One Sunday, shortly after the liquidation of the Latvian ghetto police, the inmates of the Latvian ghetto were ordered to line up in front of the *Kommandantur.* The wild rumors that began to circulate through the entire ghetto almost at once, were so terrible that the German Jewish inmates were actually relieved when they learned the reason for the order: The Latvian Jews were to hand over all their money to the German authorities. Until that time, the Latvians had been permitted to keep whatever money they possessed and to spend it as they chose, unlike the German Jews, who had never been allowed that privilege and were liable to the death penalty if caught with cash on their persons. When they had first arrived in Riga, the Jews from the Reich had been told that they would not be able to keep the money they had brought with them because it consisted of *Reichsmarks,* while the occupation currency in the Baltic States was the *Ostmark.* It is logical to assume that the Germans did not care to have another bookkeeping task on their hands, especially when they could profit by confiscating the money that the German Jews had brought along. Now, by making the Latvian Jews give up their money, too, the German authorities evidently meant to show that they no longer considered the two ghettos as separate autonomous units but thought of them as one entity, although they were still divided by a physical barrier.

It is interesting to note that in all the other ghettos of eastern Europe the Jews were permitted to have money; in some cases special money (*Judengeld*) was printed for their use. The Riga Ghetto, however, was probably considered too small for such special privileges. The Germans therefore treated the people of the Riga Ghetto, at least in this respect, like concentration camp inmates, who also were not allowed to have money in their possession.

Christmas came, and those to whom the holiday had meaning saw at least one of their wishes fulfilled. The ghetto received chicken as a Christmas treat! It smelled a little gamy because it was not quite fresh any more, but it was considered a special treat and not one person became ill. It was said to have come from the Swedish Red Cross. No matter where it came from, most of the inmates enjoyed it as a great feast.

A few weeks after Christmas, 1942, Krause was transferred to Poland. Several conflicting versions have circulated about his fate. In the list of Nazi criminals who operated in the Baltic countries, he is marked as having been killed sometime during 1943. But in Gerda Gottschalk's memoirs, which for the most part are reliable, there is a notation to the effect that Krause, though no longer commandant, was still in the Riga Ghetto as late as September, 1943, when Guenther Fleischel, the group elder, died and that he had three salvos fired at the funeral to salute his old friend. There are also depositions by former inmates stating that Krause was present at the final "selection" in the ghetto on November 2, 1943.

The salvos fired for Fleischel were heard by everyone in the ghetto, and there is little doubt that no one but the self-willed Krause could have ordered such a tribute for a

Jew. His successor, Eduard Roschmann, colorless and inept, could never have had such an unheard of idea. Furthermore, the possibility that Roschmann, and not Krause, had presided over the November "selection," is hardly likely, for Lange considered Roschmann too incompetent to preside over such a task.

Obersturmfuehrer Roschmann, formerly a lawyer in Graz, Austria, was made commandant of the ghetto in January, 1943. He either could not or would not mete out "justice" on the spot as Krause had done. In most cases, he sent offenders to the Central Prison. It was said in the ghetto that he did so not because of any qualms that he might have had but simply because he was unable to shoot straight. In *The Odessa File,* Forsythe calls Roschmann "the butcher of Riga," without so much as mentioning Lange, the real butcher, and he relegates the sadistic Krause to the job of Roschmann's deputy, another glaring inaccuracy.

One can assume that Eduard Roschmann was a murderer. He had to be to have risen that high in the SS, and indeed there was at least one murder in which he participated for certain: he, together with Gymnich and Migge, killed Max Kaufmann's son Arthur and two other young Latvian Jews. But it would be a mockery to single out Roschmann as a "butcher" and to ignore all the others. Roschmann, whose death occurred in August, 1977, lived for the preceding twenty years in South America and probably preened himself in front of his SS cronies while citing *The Odessa File* as proof of his ruthless efficiency in Riga three decades earlier. Actually, however, he was hardly a "mass murderer." The atrocities mentioned in *The Odessa File* occurred long before he came on the scene. What he actually did was much less exciting: He would spend hours on end just standing in front of the *Kommandantur,* not knowing what to do with himself. From time to time he would sneak a look inside the ghetto hospital, but mostly he would walk around aimlessly, growing fatter by the day, more or less ignored by everyone.

The great majority of the ghetto inhabitants were aware of the fact that Krause was no longer commandant and that another had taken his place, but it did not really matter to them. All they knew was that for the moment the ghetto was quiet and there were no hangings or shootings. Life was interrupted by only an occasional natural death or by news that someone had been sent either to the ghetto jail or to the Central Prison because he had been caught breaking regulations. People could live almost undisturbed as long as they made sure not to get caught committing some "illegal" act. Yet, one had to break rules sometimes and to outwit one's persecutors if one wanted to remain alive.

At the end of 1942, the two ghettos were reported to be supplying a total labor force of 6,994 males and 3,664 females to the various German army establishments and factories in Riga. According to the same report, another 40,000 workers were still needed. During the summer, the army had already complained that Jewish workers were being used as farm laborers when they were so badly needed in the munitions plants. (No complaints, however, were registered about the extermination of Jews that was taking place at the same time in the forest adjoining Camp Salaspils.)

As an example of what they considered wrong, the army high command cited one "outside" labor detail consisting of fifty young women; these women, it was pointed out, had been put to work as cleaning women and waitresses for sick officers who had been sent to the seashore to recuperate. It seemed that one branch of the army was "jealous" of another branch just because it had been able to obtain those precious Jews for its own needs. The SS alone never had cause for complaint, for their institutions always got the Jews they wanted; it was clear that the SS wielded considerable power.

Even though Jews were mainly used for work, skilled or unskilled, they were sometimes utilized for another purpose:

as subjects for medical experiments. Riga was no exception in this respect. In 1942, experiments were started to learn more about spotted typhoid fever, which was known to be transmitted by body lice. Dr. Abhagen of the Institute of Medical Zoology in Riga asked permission to cut the working hours of "his" Jews. Instead of working the prescribed minimum of eight hours per day, he asked that they be made to work no more than four hours a day, so that they might recover faster and be ready all the sooner to serve again as blood donors for his laboratory lice. His request was granted.

Later on, experiments were also performed at Camp Kaiserwald. These, too, had to do with spotted typhoid fever. The human guinea pigs from Kaiserwald, consisting of several pairs of twins, were sent away to their death with the last "selection" there, in July, 1944. As for Dr. Abhagen's "patients," they simply disappeared, and their fate was never recorded.

Within the ghetto itself, some work was done for the German army and air force. The *Gewerbebetrieb*, where all clothing and personal effects had been sorted after the "Duenamuende" massacre, no longer served that purpose. Instead, it had become a place where uniforms were mended and army furs repaired. Elderly women were put to work darning heavy army socks so that German soldiers would not freeze at the front. For the most part, the people working at these new tasks were the same who had been employed in the *Gewerbebetrieb* before the change, provided of course, that they were still alive. All new workers assigned to the *Gewerbebetrieb* after the change had to be adept at sewing or at fur work. Most of the fur workers were men.

Employment at the *Gewerbebetrieb* did not afford any opportunities for bartering. Nevertheless, it had certain advantages. Because it was an "inside" assignment, it did not entail the long treks to and from the place of work which taxed the strength of those employed at outside labor details.

Moreover, the German officer in charge at the *Gewerbebetrieb* was easy to get along with and saw to it that the place was kept well heated. The only excitement was provided by occasional searches, that kept the prisoners on their toes but did not deter them from smuggling out various items of clothing here and there.

After the *Gewerbebetrieb* no longer served as the processing center for the clothing of the dead, Camp Salaspils and several small stationary labor details in the city continued to receive a steady supply of such items until late fall of 1942. Depositions from survivors, as well as existing documents, show that transports for the Reich and occupied territories stopped coming to Riga on a regular basis in November of that year. Gestapo lists of Jewish deportees compiled after that date are usually marked "Destination Auschwitz." The environs of Riga, as well as other extermination centers in eastern Europe, were no longer needed. Auschwitz was more centrally located and had far more effective facilities for the elimination of the Jews.

One special last transport arrived in Riga in March, 1943. It consisted of a contingent of 450 men, none of them Jewish, who until then had been prisoners at the notorious concentration camp of Buchenwald and had been brought all the way east to build Camp Kaiserwald. These political prisoners and "professional criminals" were given the task of seeing to it that the Jews, who were to join them at a later time, toed the line and had experts to "teach" them about life in a concentration camp. When they arrived at the site of the new camp, they found approximately fifty Jews, who had lived there since November, 1942, clearing the ground for the barracks. These Jews left as soon as the contingent from Buchenwald arrived.[47]

The ghetto inmates were blissfully unaware of the changes that lay in store for them. They only noticed that the labor shortage in Riga was acute, for suddenly, so-called

Sprungkommandos (special labor details on call) were organized. The men who had worked hard all week long were informed one Saturday night by the house commander that they would also have to go to work the next day, Sunday, not at their regular places of employment but at other pressing jobs such as building and finishing roads, loading and unloading ships in Riga's busy harbor, clearing forests for still more roads needed by the army, and in that way, contributing even more to the war effort. In due time, women were given similar orders but never so extensive as those given to the men.

Even though the workload increased, the rations remained the same, so that the loss of the one weekly day of rest further sapped the energies of the ghetto population. Nevertheless, the inmates did not give way to despair; it seemed positively foolish to give up hope now, when it was obvious that the German army was no longer doing well on the eastern battlefront. And so, throughout that second winter, the men and women of the ghetto continued their struggle to keep alive.

Even though the transports continued to be dispatched during 1942, as early as June of that year SS Chief Heinrich Himmler had given orders to the *Einsatzgruppen* that there should not be a trace left to show what had happened to the Jews in the forests outside Riga and other cities. Accordingly, plans were made for the formation of special labor details to obliterate the evidence in places where mass slaughter had occurred.

In Riga, this labor detail would be known as *Kommando Stuetzpunkt,* with the *Sicherheitsdienst,* commanded by Lange, in charge. There was much work to be done, but Lange had to wait for spring when the ground would not be frozen anymore. The members of this detail had to exhume the bodies, build up cremation pyres, stack the bodies in a most efficient manner, and then set fire to them. Yet they were never working well and quickly enough to conceal the crimes that had been perpetrated. Moreover, as soon as the men had gained some experience, they were killed off and replaced by inexperienced workers. Unobtrusively, at first from the ghetto and later from Camp Kaiserwald, every few weeks or so, ten men would be taken away and never seen again. Suspicions were aroused, but the SS always used new ruses and in this way was able to obtain new victims easily. It was from outsiders, either civilians or German army drivers, that the Jews first heard the truth about the grisly work that was being done in the forest.

In February, 1943, it became known that the German army had suffered a great defeat at Stalingrad. Hopes revived that were further nourished by unguarded comments from German army personnel. Many people began to make plans for what they would do once they had regained their freedom, but most of them could not think further than of warmth, frequent hot baths, and good food, preferably in enormous quantities.

In the meantime, the daily struggle for survival took its toll, and the winter months again brought an increase in deaths. One reason for this was the hated Sunday work; the other was the sad fact that most people had very little to supplement their rations because they had already bartered away all their possessions.

Nevertheless, there were some who, evidently through good connections, received items they could barter outside the ghetto for food. But sometimes there was trouble; occasionally the SS would make spot checks of people returning to the ghetto from work and then, no matter how scarce the food and the barter goods, the unfortunates would throw away the precious food rather than be caught with it and punished. Later the food would be gathered up where it had been dropped and given to ghetto policemen or other Jewish administrative personnel; a few times, on orders from none other than Commandant Roschmann, it was sent to the ghetto hospital. Luckily, these searches were only sporadic, for there was a decided decrease in the amount of contraband food being brought in. Firewood, too, was at a premium and could actually be bartered inside the ghetto.

None of these shortages seemed to matter, however, when group elder Fleischel decided to give a party. The end of March, 1943, marked exactly one year since he had become the elder of the combined Berlin, Hanover, and Vienna groups, and a celebration seemed in order. There was the finest food that one could think of, including delicious cakes and cookies, as well as wine and vodka. There was dancing to a live band all night long. It was the most magnificent party any of the people present had ever given or attended in the ghetto. The source of food and liquor was not made known, but Fleischel and the other ghetto notables had had adequate opportunities to acquire it by barter. The baking went on in the ghetto all week long before the party. The finished products were then sent to the three large rooms where the Berlin group had its school. Roschmann most certainly knew about the party, but being so unlike his predecessor, he did not make an appearance, and his absence made the party even more successful.

Fleischel was the perfect host. He danced with even the most insignificant functionary and charmed everyone. Only much later, in the fall of that year, did it become clear that he had known then that he was ill and would probably never get well. When he rose to speak, he exhorted those present to have patience and never give up hope. He closed his speech by quoting a popular song which ended with a verse to the effect that every December must be followed by May. He received a standing ovation.

The words he had spoken, the coming of another spring, the news of German defeats on all battlefronts, and last but not least, the fact that they had been able to hold out that long, rekindled hope and optimism among the dwindling population of the Riga ghetto. It seemed that freedom was just around the corner.

11
Summer: 1943

Early in 1943, SS Chief Heinrich Himmler decided to do away with the entire ghetto system that had been set up in eastern Europe and to transfer the ghetto inmates to concentration camps to be built nearby. Himmler made this decision on the advice of Ernst Kaltenbrunner, the successor of Reinhard Heydrich.* Kaltenbrunner thought that the contacts between Germans and Jewish women were too close and that too many Jews were employed in confidential positions. Both Himmler and Kaltenbrunner may also have thought that conditions in the ghettos, where, as distinct from the concentration camps, families were permitted to live together and the inmates enjoyed a certain degree of autonomy, were too "good" and thus failed to accomplish the process of "destruction by means of hard labor" which had been outlined as part of the "Final Solution" at the Wannsee Conference. It seemed that as long as Jews were not killed outright, they managed to hang onto life even under the harshest conditions. Another reason for liquidating the ghetto system might have been the fear of large-scale uprisings, such as the one that had occurred in the Warsaw Ghetto in April, 1943.

Plans for a proper site for a concentration camp in the suburbs of Riga had been made as early as March. Camp Kaiserwald was being built with the idea of bringing together

---

*Heydrich, who had acquired notoriety as "The Hangman" of Nazidom, had been assassinated on June 5, 1942.

the Jews from the combined Riga Ghetto, as well as those from all "outside" labor details who had been living at their places of work. It was understood that only the strongest individuals would be sent to the new camp. The rest, those who were already too weak, or those who had been overlooked at previous "selections," or those who had been employed at various jobs inside the ghetto because of age, would then be liquidated.

The transfer of the Jews from the ghettos to the camps would entail a separation by sex, for in all the German concentration and labor camps, males and females lived in separate quarters. This separation was demoralizing and was designed to break the spirit of the inmates.

No one in the Riga ghetto could even guess at this new horror. There had been no mass execution since October, 1942; each worker seemed to be at a premium. News had been received about other ghettos in the Baltic region: Kovno and Libau (Liepaja) too, seemed destined to go on forever. The official Nazi newspaper, *Voelkischer Beobachter* reported a spring offensive by the German army, but the account sounded rather subdued and only served to raise more hopes of eventual Allied victory. With the advent of spring, the ghetto had once more experienced an awakening.

As in the year before, open-air concerts were in vogue. Of necessity, they started later in the afternoon and lasted until dusk; in that way, even those who had to work on Sundays had a chance to attend the musical programs.

Attendance at the few remaining schools had dropped considerably. It had been decided that all children aged twelve and over should be put to work either in the city or inside the ghetto where they worked mainly in the vegetable gardens. Some were used as messengers.

In the three groups administered by Fleischel, there were about thirty-five single young men whose parents had either died a natural death or had been sent away to Duenamuende.

Following the example of the Bielefeld group, Fleischel decided to open a special house as living quarters for these men and supply them with a housekeeper and a cook so that they would not have to bother with housework themselves. He received permission from the ghetto commandant to have one more building on Moskauer Strasse opened and officially added to the quarters for the combined groups. It was a home for men only, called Herrenhausen, recalling the beautiful ducal residence in Hanover, a city from which Fleischel and many of the Jews under his supervision had come.

As he had done once before in March, 1943, Fleischel decided to give another big party, which was also attended by the ghetto notables. The young men who were moving into the new house were quite happy, for there would be service personnel, freeing them from the housework that they disliked. Again Fleischel spoke, but this time he did not say that every December must be followed by May, for here it was May already and nothing had happened—nothing at all. He counseled more patience and alluded to freedom, raising his glass in a toast to survival.

Meanwhile, the ghettos of Poland were being liquidated in accordance with Himmler's schedule. No one in Riga knew about the Warsaw Ghetto uprising, and in retrospect, it probably would not have made any difference. There were some striking changes in the behavior of the SS, but they were not interpreted correctly. Starting around Easter, there was a tightening of security. The searching of labor details returning to the ghetto at the end of the day, which had been done only sporadically, was now pursued with new vigor. People attributed such zealous behavior to the change in weather. They surmised that the SS had not wanted to conduct searches during the winter months because they did not like to work outdoors in the cold. However, the suspicions of the inmates should have been aroused when the SS began to behave rather oddly: more often than not, the SS now permitted the Jews to keep the crusts of bread or the soup that they had brought back with them into the ghetto, and did not even make remarks as they had always done when they had detected such "contraband." Some inmates continued to throw away or quickly consume their "illegal nourishment" at the ghetto gate to avoid being caught, but the Germans were far more lenient about such things than they had even been before.

Many people felt that this change had something to do with Roschmann, the new ghetto commandant. He was often present when the searches were made. In reality, the searches themselves were now different; The SS resorted to frisking people, which sometimes proved embarrassing. Evidently, they were searching for something other than contraband, given the events in Warsaw and at other less well-publicized locations, they must have been looking for concealed weapons. But if that was indeed their objective, they were searching in vain, for at that time there was no thought of an armed Jewish resistance in Riga—at least not in the German ghetto. Although the episode of October, 1942 was still fresh in everyone's memory, most of the German Jews felt that the death of these forty-one Latvian Jewish heroes had been tragic, of course, but otherwise of little consequence. What would be done with the murderers once the war was over, that was quite another matter!

A conspicuous change occurred in the attitude of the young people. They became hedonistic. It seemed as if they were trying to get what they could while there was still time. There was no more talk of Zionism: it seemed so pointless. Differences between them and their parents and other members of the older generation became more pronounced. Spiritual values were scoffed at. Only the dances kept on, with a more feverish undercurrent, a hectic straining that expressed a preoccupation with the few pleasures the ghetto could offer, a frantic wish to live fast and dangerously before the end came.

At the same time, they spoke of survival. They spoke of it with ludicrous certainty even though many of them did not believe the words that came out. It was an act of bravado, trying to seem invincible. Youths working for *Einsatz-kommando 2C,* who lived outside the ghetto and visited on Sundays, shared the feeling that they had come too far to give up now, even though they were still sorting the effects of victims long gone by then. Coupled with such wishful thinking, among the young at least, there was the frenzied effort to enjoy life without a care, to get the most out of everything before it was too late.

Among the visitors to the ghetto were three young Jews who had been brought to Riga from the ghetto of Lodz with a unit of *Organization Todt,* the German Army Engineering Corps. These three Polish Jews had first established contact with the Jews from the *Reich* and from Latvia when the ghetto labor detail, called *Baugruppe Giessler,* was attached to the Engineering Corps. At the time, these were the only Polish Jews in the city. It was from their accounts that the inmates of the Riga ghetto first learned about life in the ghetto of Lodz. It was quite obvious that conditions in Riga were far better.[48]

A transport from Kovno, which earlier had been brought into the Latvian ghetto, had confirmed the impression that life in the Riga Ghetto was also far better than in Kovno. It had become apparent that the German part of the Riga Ghetto was quite unique. Thus, the German Jews were reinforced in their belief that they were indeed important and had less to fear than their fellow Jews of eastern European origin. They felt that if they did their jobs properly and obeyed orders, as befitted German Jews, they and the ghetto would be able to go on until the day of freedom arrived. Earlier doubts were not forgotten but were simply pushed aside. Pessimism was not tolerated. Sadness over past losses could be borne as long as there was hope for the future. People shouted angrily at anyone who dared to voice a doubt; they pointed to the obvious achievements of the ghetto Jews and the undeniable fact that every inmate was of great value to the German war machine.

Influenced perhaps by their Latvian counterparts, many of the German Jews developed a fondness for Degvins, the local variety of vodka, that was skillfully smuggled into the ghetto. There were some people who traded even their bread rations for it in an effort to forget their troubles for a few hours. The vodka was offered to guests who visited on Sundays or in the evenings after work. Such visits were not always of a purely social nature; they often were concerned with the bartering done during the day, but more often than not, business and pleasure were combined. There was a spirit of sharing, even if frequently there was very little one could offer to guests. Visiting in cramped quarters required cooperation from those with whom one shared one's lodgings, but that was usually no problem, for one could always reciprocate in kind.

The summer of 1943 saw an increase in food rations, with occasional extra portions given to those who worked on Sundays. The distribution of extra food was considered another hopeful sign. But although no one suspected it, the fact was that the end of the ghetto was near.

Compared with other ghettos in eastern Europe, with the exception of Kovno and Lodz, the liquidation of the Riga Ghetto occurred at a rather slow pace. It began late in May, 1943, and was not completed until November of that year. It was done in a very gradual fashion. By contrast, the emptying of other ghettos, such as Vilno, Liepaja, Minsk, Cracow, and others, usually took from three to six weeks at the most.

In Riga, plans had been made by the German authorities as early as April, 1943, to send large contingents of Jews to work in the numerous peat bogs of Latvia. As soon as it got warmer, these plans were put into effect. Starting at the end of May, people, at first only in small numbers, were sent out of the ghetto to the peat bogs where living accommodations had been prepared for them.

Factories that were not classified as essential to the war effort, simply ceased to exist as employers of Jews. Inmates who had been working there and were now suddenly and unexpectedly unemployed, were the first to go to Camp Kaiserwald. In that new camp, at a suburb of Riga called Mezapark, the men were separated from the women, and they were consigned to live in wooden barracks under conditions that made life in the ghetto seem idyllic indeed.

The manner in which the ghetto inmates first learned about the change was shocking in itself. They reported to their labor details on Prager Strasse one morning, expecting to be escorted to their place of work as usual. But when they arrived at the gate, they were met by labor detail administrator Herbert Schultz, or by his assistants, Baum or Schiff, who calmly told them that the contracts governing their employment had been canceled. In many such instances, the Jewish inmates were able to see their Latvian or German factory foreman arguing outside the gate, furious that "his" Jews were not going to be let out to go with him.

The next step was one that each inmate had dreaded ever since it became clear that it might signal the end of their lives. They were ordered to go home, pack, and report at Tin Square at a specified time the next day for "transfer to another camp."

The first such transport left the ghetto on a very hot day in July, 1943. Notwithstanding the heat, the travelers had put on three or four sweaters and sometimes a coat as well, because they remembered that there had been a time when they had been left only with what they wore on their backs. They had to walk to their destination, which was 10 kilometers away. Bundled up in their odd assortment of clothing in the great summer heat, they presented a shocking spectacle as they marched through the main thoroughfares of the city. The burden of their heavy layers of clothing in the extreme heat, coupled with the exertion of the walk, made even the strongest among them feel faint. All along the way, whenever they passed locations where Jews worked, they begged for water and very often managed to get some. Their German and Latvian SS escorts raged at those who brought out the water. The Jewish policemen and group elder Fleischel, who also walked with them to the new camp but then returned to the ghetto, recognized some of the daring good Samaritans and scolded them, saying that their behavior had been foolhardy and could have provoked the nervous SS into opening fire on the entire transport.

The fact that they were being marched in the direction of Mezapark and not toward the dreaded forest, plus the fact that Fleischel and the Jewish ghetto police had actually seen Camp Kaiserwald and had returned to tell about it, once again raised the hopes of the inmates. It seemed proof that this time, at least, the Germans did not intend to kill them but had told the truth when they had informed them that they would merely be transferred to another camp. They feared that life at the new camp would be hard; nevertheless, they were prepared to endure it as long as the Germans would permit them to remain alive.

There had apparently been some criticism in the city about the sorry picture these marchers had presented. After another two transports had been marched through the city in the same manner, all subsequent transports made the trip in trucks, presumably the same trucks that had been used as death vehicles only a year earlier.

While these transfers were taking place, political news from the outside world once more eclipsed the changes that were taking place in the ghetto. In fact, people became so excited that they were warned not to congregate in groups and discuss politics. The news of Italy's defection from the Axis camp was indeed welcome, even though Austrian and German Jews who had fought on the Italian front during World War I, were heard to mutter that "one could never trust these Italians." Fleischel and the other group elders found it necessary to call their respective groups together and appeal to them not to parade their happiness in such an obvious way when discussing the fall of Benito Mussolini. After all, one never knew who might be around the corner and overhear them. Besides, the Latvian guards could always look over the barbed-wire fence and draw their own conclusions.

The summer of 1943, that last summer in the ghetto, was truly beautiful. The foliage of the vegetable gardens promised an even more abundant yield than that of the year before. Several of the groups had built public baths, which were very popular even though they contained only a very primitive kind of shower and perhaps one bathtub. Only the Latvian ghetto had a real public bath with several showers. Nevertheless, people in the German ghetto could now occasionally take a shower after work, instead of having to make contortions inside their small washbasins.

Rations continued to improve. Horsemeat was given out more frequently; a few times the diet was enriched by oatmeal, stale but edible. It was hard to contemplate leaving the ghetto. But now even some of the more important labor details working for the army and air force were abolished and gradually, these people, too, were sent to Kaiserwald.

Some of the managers of the more important war plants had received assurances from the Nazi authorities that their Jewish workers would be permitted to return to them once the transfer to new living quarters had been completed. Those workers, much relieved at the news, thereupon smuggled their belongings out of the ghetto and stored them at their places of work, hoping to reclaim them once they were settled in their new quarters. Some were lucky. Unfortunately, however, some of the people who returned to their places of work from Kaiserwald, found to their dismay that their belongings had disappeared. In some cases, despite the promises made by the authorities, the factories did not get their workers back, and the workers never saw their possessions again. Actually, it did not make much difference, since all the belongings that the inmates took with them were confiscated once they arrived at Kaiserwald. Shortly after their arrival there, the newcomers were ordered to undress and go through a procedure called "delousing," even though they had no lice at all. When they were told that they could dress again, they found that instead of their own relatively good clothing which they had preserved so carefully over the years in the ghetto, they were given tattered, ill-fitting rags to put on.

All along, the Jewish administrators of the ghetto had tried to arrange to have the single people leave first. In effect, this meant that the Latvian Jews were the first to go. They were sent to the peat bogs as well as to the new camp in greater numbers than the German Jews. In the German ghetto, when one member of a family suddenly found himself unemployed, he was not separated from his family but would leave with the other members after all of them had lost their jobs. Moreover, until they got orders to leave, the unemployed would be given the jobs of those who had already been sent to Kaiserwald.

Before long the ghetto had few administrators. As its population decreased, some of the functionaries were transferred to Kaiserwald along with their charges, but most of them were assigned to the remaining labor details, and each day longer that one could stay in the ghetto was like a gift.

People in seasonal employment, such as work on farms or in the peat bogs, were sent directly to Kaiserwald and sometimes never even saw the ghetto again. Camp Jungfernhof, the oldest settlement of Jews from the Reich, was disbanded after the harvest, and except for fifty skilled artisans who were needed elsewhere, its inmates were sent to Kaiserwald.[49]

12
Camp Kaiserwald

By August 21, 1943, 7,874 ghetto inmates had been sent to Kaiserwald. Of that number, only 1,950 actually lived there. The others were quartered at their workplaces, such as several extremely important firms and army installations. For bookkeeping purposes, they were listed as attached to the main camp.

The Germans still did not have all the workers that they needed. Detailed plans projecting the number of inmates that would be needed at each place of work called for greater numbers of workers than the Riga ghetto was able to deliver. The German authorities, of course, knew that other Jews were expected at Kaiserwald; they knew that the surviving inmates of the ghettos of Vilno and of Libau would soon be arriving; they knew that there would be some from Kovno; but all that was still in the future. Some would finally come from as far away as Hungary via Auschwitz, yet it is safe to say that not even the German authorities knew this in 1943.

Conditions at Camp Kaiserwald, especially during those first few months of its existence, were worse than anything the prisoners had experienced before, with the exception of Camp Salaspils. The arrival itself was a traumatic event. The first impression, upon leaving the truck, was often enough to make one long for the end. The "professional criminals"—Gentiles who were serving prison terms at the camp—seemed to be stationed all over the place, shouting obscenities and beating and kicking the defenseless Jews until they had pushed them all through the gate into the camp.

Then came the lineup in front of one of the barracks and

125

the waiting for what would happen next. After all remaining possessions were taken away, they were subjected to yet another indignity: the prisoners were taken to the showers, a procedure which turned out to be both painful and complicated. First, everyone had to strip. Then, the SS men, with much relish, would examine the hair of each person for lice. At that point, there were no lice, but still, whenever they felt like it, the Nazis would order long hair on a woman cut very short, or a man's head shaved. Body hair, too, was removed, and a vile-smelling solution was smeared over armpits and pubic area. Finally came the shower, either ice-cold or scalding hot. Then, dripping wet, they would receive "new" clothes. These were all rags and invariably, the taller inmates got very short garments, while the short and skinny people almost fell out of theirs.

It was almost with a sense of relief that one finally entered the barracks. There were three barracks for women and three for men. In the beginning, two people shared one bed; the beds were arranged in two tiers. The upper bunk was not so terrible, but to be assigned the lower one was sheer torture, for the straw from the upper mattress kept falling into one's eyes and made sleep almost impossible.

Men and women were separated by two rows of barbed-wire fencing. Even though they were permitted to meet "at the fence" and talk across the separation of two yards, the professional criminals or even the SS guards often felt like disturbing the people who were so desperately trying to communicate with each other. Their tormentors would mete out slaps and beatings and would enjoy the sight of the prisoners scurrying away quickly to the safety of their barracks.

In the barracks, the lack of privacy was yet another evil. With literally no space in which to turn around, especially at the beginning, the prisoners soon became infested with lice and would frequently be seen sitting at the foot of their bunks, delousing their clothing.

But worst of all was the ceaseless harassment to which the Jewish newcomers were subjected by their Gentile fellow prisoners, not only by the professional criminals, but even by those who had been interned at the camp as political prisoners. The latter wore red triangles next to their prison numbers, identifying them as offenders against the Nazi political system as distinct from ordinary criminals; but their political quarrel with Hitler's "New Order" did not prevent them from being rabid anti-Semites. Many of them were Poles who had always hated the Jews.

Shortly before Christmas, 1943, most of the political prisoners were sent back to Germany. Camp Kaiserwald was kept mainly for Jews, supervised by the professional criminals, who were identified by green triangles sewn next to their prison numbers. They were even more cruel than the SS, if that was possible.

On the night of September 25, 1943, when two transports had arrived, one from the Riga Ghetto and one from the Vilno Ghetto, the criminal prisoners decided to give the neophytes a taste of what life would be like at Kaiserwald. They arranged what they called "a sour night," during which the Jewish male prisoners who had just arrived were forced to run around in circles inside their barracks, while their tormentors stood on the tables with clubs and whips, beating everyone who ran below them. This was kept up until the morning roll call, for which the criminals had thought up a new torture. They stood at the door and once again beat the Jews as they ran out to roll call; they seemed to be enjoying the sight of blood. From their quarters, the women heard the screams all night long but could do nothing to help their menfolk.[50]

The constant pressure, that overpowering feeling of extreme terror, as well as other, lesser indignities, broke the spirits of many who until then had been indomitable. There was no time at Kaiserwald for social amenities as there had been in the ghetto. One ceased to be a person and became just a nameless number.

The ill-nourished prisoners in their ragged clothing began to resemble scarecrows. Still, as long as the weather was warm, the lack of clothing was not a major hardship. Even the wooden-soled shoes could be endured, since labor details usually traveled in trucks rather than on foot. With a feeble attempt at humor, the prisoners would joke that they were being transported at top speed so as not to let passers-by see them and get frightened.

With the arrival of inclement weather however, many people became sick and died. Already dangerously weakened, they were unable to survive even simple colds. Eventually, coats were distributed, but this favor came too late to save many of the prisoners.

The various transports arriving at the camp, regardless of size, were always eagerly awaited by the German authorities. Invariably, there would be many personal possessions to confiscate. An especially wealthy transport arrived at Kaiserwald from the Libau Ghetto in October, 1943. After the women had been chased out of their temporary barracks, two SS men went in and brought out a big basket, filled to the brim with gold and other valuables. The bewildered women had hidden their precious belongings in the staw mattresses, believing that this temporary barrack would be their permanent quarters at Kaiserwald. The interesting fact about these Jews from Libau was that most of them spoke excellent German, which made them something like a bridge between the Jews from Riga and the German Jews. The Jews who had come from Vilno kept to themselves. Within a very short time, they managed to fill all the important positions at Kaiserwald, especially in the camp kitchen.

Theoretically, all the Jews working in and around Riga, belonged to Camp Kaiserwald. The camp itself was only a transit camp and never contained more than 2,500 prisoners at a time, except for two weeks in the summer of 1944, shortly before the retreating Germans took the first contingent of Jews "home" with them to the Reich.

In the attached outside labor camps, one or two professional criminals were placed in charge of the Jewish prisoners. The Jews did not fare much better in these subsidiary camps than at the main camp, except that the criminal overseers were often more lenient and the inmates seldom had to worry about what the next day would bring. Each day was bad, but none was worse than the other. At Kaiserwald, by contrast, the inmates could never be sure of what would happen to them next. Countless unfortunates whose only crime was that they had been caught walking from one barrack to another, were seized by the professional criminals and beaten beyond recovery. In spite of liaisons with Jewish girls, the professional criminals in the camp never stopped harassing the Jews. One could always expect a beating upon going to and from the daily labor details, during the endless roll calls, and during the "special" labor assignments that occurred on Sundays and some evenings. That particular work consisted of moving quantities of sand from one place to another, without rhyme or reason. It was backbreaking labor and sapped whatever strength the prisoners had left.

The elder of the camp was one of the professional criminals as was the administrator in charge of the labor details. At first, the barrack commanders in the men's camp were political prisoners; when they left, these jobs were assigned to professional criminals. The women's barracks were supervised by Jewish women, except for a period of about three months, during which the task was entrusted to fifty German female prisoners who had been brought to Kaiserwald from the infamous concentration camp of Ravensbrueck. Most of these women wore a black triangle next to their prison numbers, identifying them as "asocial," meaning that they had been prostitutes. They were extremely cruel to their Jewish charges and missed no opportunity to flaunt their strength and superior status. Fortunately, they lived in their own barrack.

On Christmas Eve, 1943, the women from Ravensbrueck had a big party to which all the German male prisoners were invited. Apparently, the affair turned into an orgy, because the SS felt it necessary to raid the party. The women were severely beaten and were soon sent back to Ravensbrueck. They were rather upset, but their Jewish victims were enormously relieved.

With the exception of only a few, the prisoners went to work outside the camp. Some of the smaller labor details, unlike the large ones, had a Jewish *Kapo,* as the labor detail leader was called. It was considered a lucky break to be assigned to such a detail. People on these jobs actually loved to go to their places of employment rather than stay in the camp, especially on the hated Sundays. One of these labor details was employed at the *Feldbekleidungsamt der Luftwaffe* (clothing supply office for the air force). The same Jews who had worked there while they lived in the ghetto were now brought there from Camp Kaiserwald in air force trucks, driven by German air force personnel.

The officials at the air force installation, eager to get maximum output from their Jewish workers, tried to make conditions a little easier for them. The officer in charge of the Jewish workers, *Oberzahlmeister* (chief paymaster) Hans Boos of Hanover, was so shocked at the way the Jews were dressed after having gone through that whole process at Kaiserwald, that he asked his colonel for permission to give the men blue air force coveralls and to give both men and women workers regulation air force shoes. His request was granted, although the SS insisted on painting a white cross on the back of each work outfit so that the Jews could be instantly identified. But the best part of this labor detail was that every Jewish worker got one serving of good soup each day.

The officers at some of the army installations also behaved in a relatively humane fashion toward their Jewish workers. The people reassigned to the *Armeebekleidungsamt 701* (army clothing supply center) were never even fully processed at Camp Kaiserwald. They were thus spared the customary "delousing" and all the other indignities before they were resettled at their place of work.

The best labor detail of all was the *SD Werkstaette Lenta* (Lenta security service repair shop), which was considered a veritable paradise. Besides being able to keep all the belongings that they had brought with them from the ghetto, the prisoners in this detail received good food, and the German officers in charge were surprisingly pleasant. In addition to the regular workers, many others had volunteered to go there, and the Lenta authorities were reluctant to keep them out. But in the end, Albert Sauer, the commandant of Camp Kaiserwald, threatened to close Lenta down completely if unskilled workers were not immediately taken back to the ghetto and then delivered to his tender mercies. The authorities at Lenta had no choice but to comply with his orders.[51]

The prisoners of the other outside labor camps were less fortunate. Some were even worse off than those of the main camp, because they had to work in complete isolation and thus had no chance of supplementing their meager diets by bartering. Thus, the women who worked at the *Allgemeine Elektrizitaetsgesellschaft* (A.E.G. or General Electric Corporation) were literally starving.[52] The inmates of Camp Strasdenhof, for example, were treated rather decently at first. Eventually, though, their camp achieved the dubious distinction of being the only one in the Riga area from which, in July, 1944, every person above the age of thirty was taken away and murdered.

But all this was yet to come. So was the transport of 500 women who arrived at Kaiserwald in May, 1944, from Auschwitz, where they had been brought from Budapest and other Hungarian cities only a few weeks before. Many of those who were now struggling to survive never lived to see freedom. Meanwhile, there was another winter to overcome, one which taxed the remaining survivors to the utmost.

13
The End of the Riga Ghetto

In September, 1943, the enigmatic Guenther Fleischel, group elder of the Riga Ghetto, died of cancer of the stomach. Dr. Aufrecht, the medical superintendent of the ghetto, operated on him, but it was too late. He was given a "state funeral," with his coffin borne through the streets of the ghetto, followed by his beautiful sobbing widow, dressed completely in black and heavily veiled. The functionaries who were still in the ghetto at the time also followed the coffin. The funeral was like an omen; most of the mourners felt that it truly signified the end of the ghetto. German guards were present, and at the command of Krause, who might have been in Riga for business reasons,* three volleys were fired over Fleischel's grave. It was a fitting tribute for a man who had symbolized this most unusual transplanted German community. His complex personality reflected the age-old relationship between Germany and its Jews. The three volleys were Krause's instinctive acknowledgement of that peculiar phenomenon.

The ghetto was emptying at a fast rate now. Shortly after the funeral, Fleischel's widow, together with her sister and brother-in-law, was sent to a labor detail. She survived, and after the war, resumed her maiden name and remarried.

While the identification numbers assigned to Jews at Camp Kaiserwald had started with 500, the numbers were now well

---

*Krause was said to have an interest in "Farmacija," a wholesale drug firm in Riga.

133

over 8,000. Everyone had to wear his or her number on the left side of the chest, exactly where the yellow Star of David had been worn before. The Star of David had been replaced by a yellow triangle next to the number.

The ghetto of Riga had become very quiet indeed. Several times during the month of October, the stillness was broken by trucks that rolled in from Kaiserwald, bringing back the sick. These "casualties" were dispatched to the ghetto hospital; those who recovered were sent back to Kaiserwald. Those who showed no improvement after a few days, were temporarily left in the ghetto and could be seen sitting in the sunshine, often unable to rouse themselves from their stupor, even when Commandant Roschmann walked by. Knowing well what was in store for them, Roschmann simply ignored them. Only a few weeks before, they had been so strong and had gone through so much without collapsing, but they had not been able to withstand the tortures of Kaiserwald.

By the third week of October, most of the inmates had been transferred out of the ghetto. On November 2, 1943, the decimated ghetto was ready for the final act. That morning the few remaining labor details, including *Armeebekleidungsamt 701,* had gone out to work as usual. When they returned to the ghetto in the evening, they found that all the older people who had been in charge of cleaning the houses, all the remaining children and their teachers, and all the ailing people, both in and out of the hospital, along with those who had been sent back sick from Kaiserwald, had been taken away. Among those removed were also functionaries of the ghetto who had asked to go along so as not to be separated from their children who were part of the transport.[53]

All these unfortunate members of the transport were not sent to the forest but to Auschwitz. Evidently, it was not thought wise to create more work for the men who were busy in the forest obliterating the traces of the mass killings that had been committed there earlier. Besides, the methods of extermination used in Auschwitz were far more efficient than those used in the forest had ever been, in that they required far less manpower and at the same time yielded more "raw materials."

There are conflicting reports concerning the number of people who were sent to Auschwitz on that day. Several depositions state the number to have been over 2,000. Even though this number suggests a rather large contingent, it does make sense if one considers that it not only contained the aged and the children but also the sick and the disabled who had been transferred back to the ghetto from Kaiserwald. Frieda Marx, who worked at the *Kommandantur*, gave the number as 2,246; Hermann Voosen, whose child was taken away that day, gave the number as 2,286. The registrar at Auschwitz, however, a Dr. Wolken, maintained that he had received only 596 persons. But he did not say whether that number constituted those left after the usual "election," whether it included only the males, or whether it excluded those who had died en route.

After a few more days in what was now a veritable ghost town, all those still in the ghetto were sent out, either to Camp Kaiserwald or to *Armeebekleidungsamt*. As they left, they could see small columns of people arriving in the ghetto. Approximately 120 Jews who up to that time had still been working in several small labor details outside the ghetto and had lived at their places of work, were being returned to the ghetto where they were all assigned to living quarters in one building. Their job was to clean up after those who had left. They were ordered to search the empty apartments for items that could be salvaged for transfer to the Reich; they then assorted and repaired the clothing left behind by the deportees, packed it, and loaded it onto waiting trucks.

The life of the inmates assigned to the cleanup detail was an easy one. Commandant Roschmann, hardly ever bothered them. They were able to obtain enough food through barter at the Skirotava Station to which they brought the packaged goods for shipment to the Reich. They even had entertainment in the person of the violinist Brandt, formerly of the Latvian ghetto, who, with his Viennese "wife," Margit had entered into a "ghetto marriage" a year before and now could finally live together undisturbed. Their idyll was to last until August 8, 1944, the day when the oceanliner *Bremen* landed in Danzig and unloaded the pitiful contingent of Jews from the Baltic states brought back to the Reich. There, on a meadow, waiting to embark in barges for Stutthof, Brandt, for the last time, serenaded his wife and all the others, playing "J'attendrais," not realizing that only a handful would live to see freedom and that neither he nor his wife would be among them. But that poignant moment belonged to the future, and in the meantime, the people in this labor detail, most of whom were younger than the Brandts, lived only from one day to the next.[54] Every few weeks or so, their number was reduced when a small detail of men would be removed from the ghetto. Since these men never arrived at Camp Kaiserwald, it must be assumed that they were sent to the forest to replace members of the burial detail who were periodically exterminated so that they would not live to tell what they had seen. Later events proved that the Germans could have saved themselves the trouble; there was not enough time to get rid of all the evidence. A State Emergency Commission appointed by the Russians after their reoccupation of Riga in October 1944, found several mass graves as well as fuel barrels in the Bikernieki Forest. At other sites, the cleanup work had never even begun.

By July, 1944 there were about sixty persons left in the Riga Ghetto, twenty man and forty women. From all appearances, they had completed their task satisfactorily—it had taken less than a year to remove all traces of the former inhabitants. And so their work having been accomplished, they were put on trucks and were finally taken to Camp Kaiserwald.

The ghetto was empty.

Epilogue

Thirty-five years have passed, and the survivors of the German ghetto of Riga remember it as a harsh place, but not as an impossible one to live in compared to what came later. Most of them, during numerous personal interviews, seemed aware of how different their experiences had been from those of the survivors of other ghettos. Their wistful reminiscence was no doubt influenced by the fact that most of them still had their families with them at the time.

While they well remember the cold, the hunger, and other physical discomforts, they also point with pride to the institutions they had been able to establish in the ghetto, the schools, the theaters, the concerts, and the sports events. They proudly recall that they had succeeded in establishing, even in the ghetto, a society where ethical standards were scrupulously observed.

They maintain that they tried to comply with the orders given to them by the ghetto authorities and that existing rules were obeyed whenever possible. Of course, regulations pertaining to smuggling food and stealing other vital articles had to be ignored for the sake of survival. Stealing was commonly referred to as "organizing" and it can be argued that the inmates of the ghetto only "stole back" the items that had been taken from them. But the very fact that they felt compelled to use a euphemism to describe their "illegal" acts, points to their middle-class desire for respectability.

They realize that they had become callous in the ghetto. One could not get very excited about death when death was so commonplace. On the other hand, they are aware of the fact that records of natural deaths, suicides, and "selections" were kept, with the Nazis getting one set of records and the Jews retaining another set for use after the war. However, when the ghetto was liquidated in November, 1943, those records, too, were destroyed. It was impossible for the Jews to take them along.

Many people kept diaries; some managed to smuggle them to Kaiserwald and even to Camp Stutthof.* These diaries, important as they are as the only available records, were mostly of a personal nature and not intended as documentaries. Also, tragically, the people who, by virtue of their age and education might have been expected to remember at least important data, did not survive the war.

When discussing their apparent inability to perceive the reality of the "Final Solution," survivors mention that the ghetto had seemed to them like home, a place where correct behavior was still prized, where titles, such as *Herr Doktor* and *Professor* were used not only among the inmates to each other, but by many of the German authorities as well, and where one's social status of former days was still an important factor. There was, naturally, a so-called ghetto elite, but since their power was minimal, they were not regarded with awe, unless they had been known as people of substance back home.

To understand the earlier refusal of the inmates of the German ghetto to accept the atrocities committed upon the Latvian Jews as an intimation of their own prospects, one must consider two things: first, that the human mind often cannot assimilate inconceivable realities, and second, that the German Jews had been made to believe that "it" could only happen to the *Ostjuden,* but never to them.

---

*Stutthof, a concentration camp located about 35 kilometers east of Danzig, was set up in September 1939. In the fall of 1944, it received Jews from the Latvian camps and from Auschwitz. Of the 52,000 prisoners who had passed through Stutthof by the end of the war, only about 3,000 survived.

After March 15, 1942, there was ample evidence that the Jewish deportees from Germany had no cause to consider themselves exempt from the fate that had befallen their fellow Jews in the Latvian ghetto. But even then there were those who kept pointing to the fact that "only" the old, the infirm, and the children had been singled out for extermination and that strong, healthy individuals like themselves would be safe from harm, perhaps not because they were German, but because their work was so important to the war effort.

Some, of course, intellectually accepted the truth even though they refused to acknowledge it emotionally. They found it very difficult, even impossible, to convey these realities to their fellow inmates. As experts on the Holocaust have repeatedly pointed out, the Nazis used the technique of the "big lie" to induce their victims to go to their deaths quietly, like sheep to the slaughter. It was much easier to believe the "big lie," and in Riga it was extremely successful.

The attitude of the German Jews toward the individuals who superintended them should be of considerable interest to students of the Holocaust. The inmates of the German Jewish ghetto felt that most of the Jewish ghetto officials had treated them fairly; indeed, they say that they trusted and even respected some of them. As for the Nazi officials, everyone had hated and feared *Obersturmbannfuehrer* Lange. Feelings toward the original commandant of the ghetto, Kurt Krause, had been ambivalent. As for Roschmann, Krause's successor, most of the inmates had hardly been aware of him, and the survivors are somewhat bemused by the prominence accorded to him in *The Odessa File.* For the Latvian SS guards, on the other hand, the inmates of the German Jewish ghetto had nothing but contempt. This attitude signifies the ethnocentricity of the German Jews, even in a Nazi ghetto; they despised the Latvians not only because of their eagerness to help the German Nazis effect the "Final Solution," but also because they, the Jews of German origin, considered the Latvian people as "inferior" and "backward."

The inmates of the Latvian ghetto perceived their situation in much more realistic terms than did their counterparts in the German ghetto. Their lives had been shattered by what had happened to their wives and children on November 29 and December 8, 1941. Whereas the inmates of the German ghetto fashioned a society for themselves, complete with cultural events, Friday night gatherings, and Zionist groups, the Latvian Jews found it impossible even to attempt to lead normal lives. While some of them eventually found personal gratification in their contacts with women in the German ghetto, this did not change their general outlook. With few notable exceptions, the inmates of the Latvian ghetto remained a society without hope.

Eventually, after the liquidation of the Riga Ghetto, the German Jews were to realize how well the Latvian Jews had understood the diabolical Nazi plan right from the start. In the death camps, they were to see at long last that in the eyes of the non-Jewish world it did not matter whether a Jew had come from the Reich or from some east European country. Once the German Jews perceived the "Final Solution" in all its true horror, most of them no longer tried to find rational explanations for the behavior of the Nazi authorities or to single out instances of relatively humane behavior on the part of the Nazis whom they had encountered. At last, it had become quite clear to them that all the Germans involved in the "settlement" of the "Jewish problem" were their implacable foes, and they felt nothing but hatred for the German overlords who had heaped so many indignities upon them.

There is a certain sense of kinship that unites all survivors of the Nazi Holocaust. But those who were together in the Riga Ghetto have perhaps achieved something more than that; they are bound together by the experience of having lived in and survived conditions unique even within the unprecedented events of the Holocaust. They survived the dreaded deportation to the east in far greater numbers than their counterparts who were sent to Lodz, Minsk, Izbitza, and Treblinka. As a matter of fact, only a handful of the German Jews survived the Lodz experience, one or two came back from Minsk, and none from any of the other extermination centers. Yet, of the 20,000 German, Austrian, and Czech Jews who had been deported to Riga during the winter of 1941-1942, approximately 800 survived. Among them were the author, her mother, and her sister.

The majority of these survivors are now living in the United States. There are several in Israel, in Australia, in England, and in Canada. Most of those who lived to see the end of the war and survived the sudden shock of liberation, went back to their hometowns to see whether any of their relatives and friends had returned. Their hopeful journeys, in most cases, turned out to be futile. Yet, a number of the survivors decided to rebuild their lives in their native countries.

The ghetto survivors had cherished hopes that with the fall of Hitler the world would somehow be changed. They thought that the end of the war would signal the advent of a new era of justice and tolerance. Many of them, however, when returning to their hometowns in search of other survivors, found that they had hardly been missed by former Gentile friends and neighbors and were shocked to find that their return was greeted by polite indifference or by outright hostility.

Vengeance seemed futile. Throughout the lengthy Nuremberg war crimes trials they had felt that here, at last, justice would be served. But the advent of the "cold war" soon dashed those hopes. Their former tormentors were able to find safe havens in all parts of the world and never received the punishment that would have befitted their crimes.

As more and more information became available to them, the survivors gradually realized the full extent of the catastrophe that had befallen their people, and they understood the efficiency which had hastened the "Final Solution." Having been part of it did not lessen their bewilderment, and the realization that their own survival was almost a miracle and not due to anything they themselves had done, only served to prolong the time that it took to regain their balance. It is a precarious one, to say the least. From time to time, when they are called upon to bear witness against those who transgressed against them, they suffer perhaps more than the perpetrators of evils.

At this point in time, the survivors of the Riga Ghetto had become integrated into the communities where they have settled since the war. For the most part, they represent a dwindling, inconspicuous element in their surroundings. Most of them live what can be described as a "good" life. Over the years, they have formed new relationships, they do their work, and they are good citizens. But most of them feel that no matter where they are living today, they will never quite cease to be "marginal" men and women in the society where fate has placed them.

They do all the things that other people do, but they have never really left the ghetto. Their memories overshadow every aspect of their lives. They cannot kiss their children without fear that they will someday lose them, too, or without remembering those other children whose lives ended in the Bikernieki or Rumbula Forests near Riga. They try to fight these depressions as well as they can by endeavoring to play constructive roles in society and by trying to help make the world a better place in which to live, even though they have their doubts about the feasibility of such an endeavor.

They realize that the world kept silent in the face of genocide. It is therefore not surprising that the survivors are skeptical and apprehensive. They are constantly on their guard, alert and watchful, and will let themselves go only when they are together with other survivors, who are equally encumbered by memories which cannot be erased. Then, and only then, no matter what the occasion, their talk turns to their ghetto, and they are back home again.

Notes

1. Frederick Forsythe, *The Odessa File* (New York: The Viking Press, 1972).

2. Howard Blum, *Wanted!* (New York: Quadrangle Press, 1976).

3. Max Kaufman, *Die Vernichtung der Juden Lettlands* (Munich: Deutscher Verlag, 1947).

4. Jeannette Wolff, *Sadismus oder Wahnsinn* (Dresden: Sachsenverlag Druckerei, 1946); Josef Katz, *One Who Came Back: (The Diary of a Jewish Survivor)*, translated from the German by Hilda Reach (New York: Herzl Press, 1973).

5. Raul Hilberg, *The Destruction of the European Jews*, with a new postscript by the author (Chicago: Quadrangle Paperback, 1967); Gerald Reitlinger, *The Final Solution: The Attempt to Exterminate the Jews of Europe 1939 - 1945*, rev. ed. (South Brunswick, New Jersey: Thomas Yoseloff, 1961).

6. Adolph Hitler, address to the Reichstag, Berlin, Germany, January 30, 1939, in *Dokumente der Deutschen Politik und Geschichte,* 5:8. He made essentially the same statement on several other occasions (January 30, 1942; September 30, 1942; February 24, 1943; March 21, 1943; and December 9, 1943). In 1939, Hitler was prophetic. However, the next time he expressed this idea, at the end of September, 1942, he had already instituted "the final solution."

7. Zenta Maurina, *Die eisernen Riegel zerbrechen* (Memmingen: Maximilian Dietrich Verlag, 1957) p. 129. Miss Maurina presents an exact description of how pleased even well-educated Latvians were about the later fate of the Jews. The author, who left her country in 1944, tried to be even-handed in her anecdotes about Jews, although some anti-Jewish bias is discernible. While her report is very detailed on horrors perpetrated by the Russians, whom she hates, she says very little about the fate of the Jews in Riga and environs, even though she was there throughout the time of their destruction.

8. Victor Arajs is awaiting trial in Germany. For these many years, he lived under his wife's maiden name. Cukurs was executed in Montevideo, Uruguay, in 1965 by a detachment of Israelis who called themselves "The Avengers." Hazners lives in baronial splendor near Albany, New York, insisting that charges against him are part of a communist-inspired plot.

9. *Tevija,* the main Latvian newspaper, July 11, 1941. The editor was Pauls Kovalivskis; Arturs Kroders was the manager. The owner of the paper met Himmler in Berlin in 1942 and assured him that there was no longer a "Jewish Problem" in Latvia.

10. Max Kaufmann, *Die Vernichtung der Juden Lettlands,* p. 85.

11. From an interview with Mara Godes, one of these survivors. New York City, May 28, 1972.

12. Kaufmann, *Die Vernichtung der Juden Lettlands,* p. 139.

13. *Ibid.,* p. 189. His exact quotation is *"es war ungeschickt, dass die lettische Jugend den deutschen Frauen so viel zu essen brachte."* The word *"ungeschickt"* is this context would mean "unwise."

14. Gestapo lists are on file at the International Tracing Service in Arolsen, Hessen. Some are still marked "Riga," evidently because that is where they were supposed to go at first. The description of the transports from the Reich is based on an interview with Ceil Welles, a survivor of the Kovno Ghetto. Their fate is also described in the *Jaeger Brief,* a report by *SS Standartenfuehrer* Jaeger to Dr. Stahlecker, detailing the various mass executions in Lithuania from July 4 to November 29, 1941.

Day of Departure	Number of Deportees	City of Departure	Destination	Date of Execution
Nov. 15	1,000	Munich	Kovno	Nov. 25
Nov. 17	943	Berlin	Kovno	Nov. 25
Nov. 22	991	Frankfurt	Kovno	Nov. 25
Nov. 23	1,000	Vienna	Kovno	Nov. 29
Nov. 23	1,005	Breslau	Kovno	Nov. 29

15. Deposition of Hans Werner Loszynski at the trial of Rudolf Seck in Hamburg, *Riga Prozess,* Akte MB/1A. See also the deposition of Mascha Katz from Lehrte, Hamburg transport.

16. From the deposition of Gerda Rose-Wasserman, Hamburg transport.

17. Latvian survivor of Camp Salaspils, Roland Jaucis, in his deposition at the Munich *Institut fuer Zeitgeschichte.* See also *IMT,* vol. VII, p. 286. There were more than 3,000 children in Salaspils.

18. Eyewitness account of Isser Lurie, whose wife and three children were killed on December 8, 1941.

19. *Bericht ueber die Evakuierung von Juden nach Riga,* dated December 26, 1941, pertaining to the transport from Duesseldorf to Riga, December 11 to 17, signed by Salitter, *Hauptmann der Schutzpolizei.*

20. From an interview with Sally Katz, the only other survivor of his family. He was liberated by the Russians in 1945. Because of his Aryan looks as well as the fact that he spoke only German, the Russians believed him to be a German spy and sent him to Siberia. He was not released until ten years later and he is now living in New York.

21. From an interview with Ludwig (Larry) Pick, the young man in charge of the mass grave. Jaffee, his former religious instructor in Stuttgart, had been assigned to bring the bodies to the grave.

22. Zdenek Lederer, *Ghetto Theresienstadt* (London: Edward Goldstone and Son, Ltd., 1953). This ghetto in Czechoslovakia was established for the "important" Jews, a so-called *"Prominenten Ghetto."* In reality, it became a transient camp, with transports leaving for eastern Europe almost every week. The author describes the two transports that went to Riga. They were classified O and P.

23. From an interview with Vera Kisch-Mausner, whose father went to Camp Jungfernhof while she and her mother were marched into the ghetto.

24. From an interview with Ruth Wilner-Roseboom, November, 1972.

25. According to Lederer, *Ghetto Theresienstadt,* p. 208, these people were taken to the forest and shot. However, during January, while Lange was in Berlin, no mass shooting took place.

26. In his deposition after the war, Hermann Voosen, a member of this group, still maintained that his was the last transport. The deposition is on file at the Wiener Library, London.

27. My family and I lived in the same apartment with the Brunn family. Old Mrs. Brunn joined the cleanup detail in February as a replacement. She brought home wood as well as other things she found, sometimes even jewelry hidden by the Latvian Jews and overlooked by Drechsler's men.

28. From a deposition given by Mrs. Sollinger, the woman in charge of labor details for the Hanover group. Her husband, Julius, was one of the ghetto policemen involved. When he came back, he told her, but they did not tell anyone else. She alone of her family survived the war and is now living in the United States.

29. From an interview with Kurt Sauerquell, New York City. In January and February of 1977, Maywald was tried by the German authorities in Hamburg. He was sentenced to four years in jail but is at this time out on bail. According to the German judge, there was "a lack of competent" witnesses, even though Kurt Sauerquell took the stand and told the court how Maywald had sent his mother to her death.

30. *Goebbels Diaries,* entry for April 24, 1942, p. 183.

31. My sister, Rita Hirschhorn-Wassermann, was the *Ordonnanz* of the *Zentral Lazarett.* She worked at the hospital every day after school. After her twelfth birthday on August 30, 1942, she worked there full time.

32. From an interview with Gerda Rose-Wasserman. She now lives in New York.

33. According to Krause's secretary, Frieda Marx, nee Meyer, in her deposition on the trial of Baltic war criminals.

34. From an interview with Kurt Roseboom, a policeman of the Berlin group, who counted the people as they entered the vans.

35. From a deposition by Mrs. Stabulniece.

36. My father, who was forty-four years old at the time, left with this last transport but returned to the ghetto on June 2. Because of the harsh conditions at Salaspils, he had lost almost twenty-five pounds during the four weeks that he was there.

37. From a deposition made by Hans Baerman of the Cologne group.

38. *Death Camp Salaspils,* p. 9. Evian Avotins, J. Dzirkalis and V. Petersons, *Daugavas Vanagi: Who Are They?* (Riga: Latvian State Publishing House, 1963), pp. 32-33. Also see the deposition of Arnold Roland Jaucis, Latvian political prisoner, at the trial of Teckemeier in Bielefeld. Lists compiled by *Juedische Gemeinde zu Berlin* are marked "Riga." French lists are marked *"nach dem Osten"* (to the east) and do not specify exact point of disembarkation. The same is true of several Czech transports, also marked *"nach dem Osten"* as quoted by Lederer, *Ghetto Theresienstadt,* pp. 215-223.

39. In 1965, the court in Riga sentenced Boleslavs Maikowskis to

death *in absentia.* He has been living in the United States since 1950, and there have been several attempts to bring him to trial.

40. Josephine died in 1944. Sally is now living in England.

41. The twins were killed in the last children's roundup in the summer of 1944. Schultz and his wife survived the war and are now living in Germany.

42. Reitlinger confuses Anton Brunner with Alois Brunner, Eichmann's right-hand man, an expert on mass deportations who "worked" in several European countries. It was Alois who shot Siegmund Bosel on February 7, 1942, on the way to Riga. He is reported to be living in Syria. Anton Brunner was hanged in Vienna in 1946.

43. In *The Odessa File,* Olly is portrayed in a different and somewhat idealized light. She is also transformed into a girl from Munich, is described as Roschmann's "concubine" and not Krause's, and, last but not least, is shown working hard to help the ghetto population.

44. Jeanette Wolff, *Sadismus oder Wahnsinn* p. 11. Her list of rations agrees with what Gottschalk quotes in her memoirs as well as with the entry in my own diary.

45. Lurie was one of a contingent of ten men taken to the forest to exhume bodies and burn them. It happened to him despite the fact that he had always been on the alert; the SS fooled him and the other nine by asking for ten men to stuff mattresses at Camp Kaiserwald in July, 1944.

46. Gottschalk, *Der Letzte Weg,* p. 28. Entry in my own diary for October 30, 1942. See also Wolff, *Sadismus oder Wahnsinn,* but note that she lists the year as 1943. By October of 1943, the Riga Ghetto was almost empty. When interviewing Wolff in Berlin in August, 1971, I told her of her error, and she realized her mistake. Because Reitlinger and Hilberg use her as a source, they also have the date wrong and connect the liquidation of the ghetto on November 2, 1943, with the armed uprising.

47. From the deposition of Ivan Brager of Hamburg who came to Riga in November, 1941. Together with seventy-two other men he was sent to what was to become Camp Kaiserwald. The remaining members of his transport were exterminated. When the Buchenwald contingent arrived, he and the other men, numbering about fifty, were sent first to

the ghetto and then to an SS repair park for trucks and other vehicles.

48. The three Polish Jews were Moses Tellmann, Abraham Goldmann, and Meyer Wilczkowski. Tellmann and Goldmann worked as tailors, and Wilczkowski as a locksmith. He was tall, blond, and blue-eyed and freely walked around the city. During a surprise check for identification papers, he was discovered, brought to the Central Prison, and eventually executed. The other two survived. Tellmann is now living in Israel and Goldmann in the United States.

49. From an interview with Victor Marx who had been sent to Camp Jungfernhof from Stuttgart and who was one of the fifty artisans. He is now living in the United States.

50. My parents and I had arrived at Camp Kaiserwald on September 25. When we saw my father in the morning, after the "sour night," we hardly recognized him. The faces of the other men who came with our contingent were also bloody and swollen, and it took several days until they resummed a normal appearance.

51. Gottschalk, *Der Letzte Weg*, p. 33. She and her sister were at Lenta, but only her sister was able to remain there. Gerda went to Strasdenhof. Her sister later died at Stutthof.

52. After the war, A.E.G. paid their former slaves a total amount of $500.00 restitution per person.

53. This information was taken from the depositions of Hermann Heymann, Selma Breitner-Feldman, and Heinz Samuel. Hermann Heymann went to Auschwitz with his family. He believes that he is the sole survivor of the entire transport. Selma Breitner-Feldman went out to work in the morning and, when she came back that evening, found that her mother, Mrs. Glattstein, was gone. Heinz Samuel says that Krause was in charge of the ghetto's liquidation.

54. Abraham Goldmann and Moses Tellmann, the two Polish Jews mentioned earlier, were part of the group cleaning up the ghetto. Several of the men were at the same time transforming the old cemetery into a park, leaving only the trees intact. When I visited the site in 1971, I found that the few remaining Latvian Jews still place candles under the trees. I also found that very few of the Latvian population ever enter the park; they say that it is haunted.

The author (left) and her sister shortly before Hitler's takeover of Austria. The two little girls served as flowergirls at their youngest uncle's wedding.

1

2

3

4

5

6

1. *Max Kaufmann, author of* The Destruction of Latvian Jewry. *2. Hertha Weiss, the girl who went to Kommandant Krause to beg for her father's life. 3. Dr. Weiss. His sentence was commuted from hanging to shooting. 4. Dolly Spiegel. Kommandant Krause let her live despite her being a smuggler. She had her hair shorn off and stood in front of the* Kommandantur, *wearing a sign which proclaimed her "crime". 5. Vera Kisch. She and her mother went to the ghetto. Her father (6.) went to Camp Jungfernhof and was part of the contingent sent to the forest for liquidation two months later. 7. Jeanette Wolff, author of* Sadismus oder Wahnsian, *member of the German Bundestag (Parliament) after the war.*

7

(Above) Barbed wire around the ghetto. The sign proclaims that anyone trying to make contact would be shot. (Left) Berliner Strasse #4. Fleischel's office.

A work kommando *on their way home to the ghetto.*

This is how Berliner Strasse looked after the massacre of the Latvian Jews.

Oberst   bannfeuhrer. *Dr. Lange decorating Victors Arays, his Latvian counterpart.*

Open mass grave in the Bikernieki Forest.

(Above) Every third person in each row was taken to the Bikernieki Forest to be shot.
(Below) Empty and half-filled fuel barrels in the Bikernieki Forest, left over from
the burning of corpses—a job which was never completed.

(Above) Victims in Salaspils. (Below) Half-filled mass grave in the Rumbula Forest.

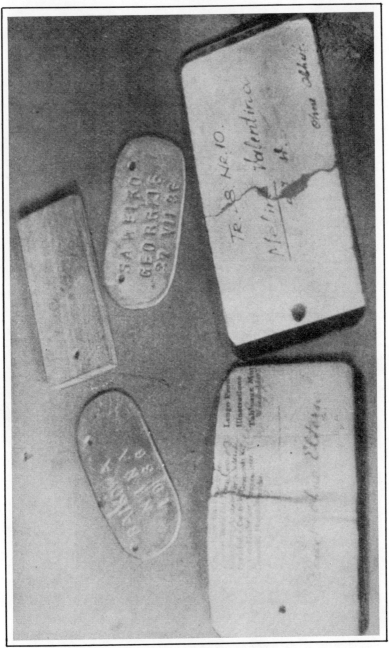

Name tags of orphaned children brought to Salaspils for extermination.

Women ready for execution. (When this picture was shown on television, two sisters now living in New Jersey recognized their mother in the center.)

(Above) In the bitter cold, the doomed victims walked toward their deaths. (Below) Huddled together waiting to be next.

(Above) Stone monument in the Rumbula Forest commemorating the two massacres during which most of the Latvian Jews were exterminated. (Below) This commemorates the barracks where experiments on children were conducted in Salaspils.

In Latvian, Russian, and Yiddish, the "victims of facism" are remembered in the Rumbula Forest.

The Vanquished.

The Savior.

Part of a memorial group of statues in Salaspils.

The Fighters.

Appendix

A
Transports from the Reich to Riga

Day of Departure	Number of Deportees	City of Departure	Destination
Nov. 27	1,000	Berlin	Rumbula Forest
Nov. 29	714	Nuernberg	Jungfernhof
Dec. 1	1,200	Stuttgart	Jungfernhof
Dec. 3	1,042	Vienna	Jungfernhof
Dec. 4	808	Hamburg	Jungfernhof
Dec. 7	1,000	Cologne	Ghetto
Dec. 9	991	Cassel	Ghetto
Dec. 11	1,007	Duesseldorf	Ghetto
Dec. 12	1,000	Bielefeld	Ghetto
Dec. 15	1,001	Hanover	Ghetto
Jan. 9	1,000	Theresienstadt	Ghetto
Jan. 11	1,000	Vienna	Ghetto and Jungfernhof
Jan. 13	1,037	Berlin	Ghetto
Jan. 15	1,000	Theresienstadt	Ghetto and Salaspils
Jan. 19	1,006	Berlin	Ghetto
Jan. 21	1,000	Leipzig	Ghetto
Jan. 25	1,051	Berlin	Ghetto
Jan. 26	1,200	Vienna	Ghetto
Jan. 27	1,000	Dortmund	Ghetto
Feb. 6	1,000	Vienna	Ghetto and Rumbula Forest
	20,057		

B
List of Survivors

Name	Transport
Abraham Hans	unknown
Adler Hertha, nee Michelsohn	Hanover
Adler Hilde, nee Weil	Cologne
Adler Josef	Berlin
Adler Julius	Kassel
Althausen Edith, nee Kugelmann	Kassel
Altschul Elvira	Prague
Apfel Emmy, nee Rosenberg	Dortmund
Apfel Guenter	Dortmund
Ardon Elieser	unknown
Aron Minna	unknown
Atlas Herta	unknown
Baehr Else, nee Franke	Bielefeld
Baerman Heinz	Cologne
Baerman Margrit, nee Kohlman	Cologne
Barnass Gerda, nee Mahler	unknown
Baruch Walter*	Cologne
Bauer Gerda, nee Samson	Bielefeld
Baum Berd	unknown
Baum Charlotte	unknown
Becher Claus	Hanover
Beer Zeev (Bully)	Berlin
Behrendt Margarete	Berlin
Behrens Henry	Nuernberg
Behrens Margot, nee Schocken*	Berlin

*Died since the liberation

157

Name	Transport
Bender Eva, nee Loewenberg	Kassel
Bennet Anne, nee Rothstein	Hanover
Berger Liesl, nee Schorr	Vienna
Bergerova Bronja, nee Berger	unknown
Berlin Chana	unknown
Berman John (Hans)	Cologne
Berner Inge, nee Gerson	Berlin
Bernheimer Alice, nee Borg	Stuttgart
Bernstein Ludvik	Prague
Bettler Edith	Vienna
Bettler Fritz	Vienna
Bieder Sonja	unknown
Billig Rudy	Cologne
Blau Meta	Bielefeld
Bloch Johanna	Vienna
Blutstein Inge, nee Ozzenheimer	unknown
Brager Ivan	Hamburg
Brandeis Renate, nee Leeser	Duesseldorf
Brandon Edith, nee Blau	Bielefeld
Brandt Erna, nee Fuchs	unknown
Briemer Rachel, nee Harf	Duesseldorf
Brill Helene, verw. Meyer-Funke	Duesseldorf
Buchheim Lore, nee Grueneberg	Dortmund
Butter Tilly	Cologne
Buxbaum Bertel, nee Ievi	Kassel
Cahn Gustel, nee Levy	Cologne
Capell Margot, nee Schwarz	Cologne
Carlebach, Rabby Salomon	Hamburg
Ceslanski Julius	Nuernberg
Charmatz Else, nee Ickenberg	Bielefeld
Cohn Marga	unknown
Cohn Miriam	unknown
Cohnen Alfred	Duesseldorf
Cohnen Grette, nee Winter	Duesseldorf

Name	Transport
Dahl Irene, nee Harf	Duesseldorf
Dahl Jacob*	Duesseldorf
Dangan Alberg*	unknown
Daniels Hannelore	Duesseldorf
Daniller Harry	unknown
De Jong Ilse	unknown
Deutsch Friedrich	Vienna
De Vertenil Hanny, nee Oppenheimer	Nuernberg
De Vries Marta, nee Marcus	unknown
Diamond Hilda	Prague
Dollefield Theodor*	Kassel
Du Bonsky Lore, nee Horn	Hanover
Durra Erwin	Berlin
Dvorskin Saja	unknown
Ehrenberg Dorothy, nee Gundelfinger	Stuttgart
Ehrichova Gerda, nee Ehrlich	Prague
Eichenwald Elly	Dortmund
Eichenwald Ruth	Dortmund
Eichhorn Bertha, nee Seiferheld	Nuernberg
Einstein Curt	Stuttgart
Engel Franziska	Vienna
Engel Karl	Vienna
Essinger Betty	unknown
Fein Lore, nee Sass	Dortmund
Feist Betty, nee Rothschild	Berlin
Feitelson, Dr. J.	unknown
Feldman Selma, verw. Breitner	Vienna
Felsen Margot, nee Stoppelman	Hanover
Felsenthal Ruth, nee Spangenthal	Kassel
Fern Lilo, nee Stern	Kassel
Field Hertha, nee Weiss	Vienna
Fiergang Ruth, nee Heymann	Dortmund

*Died since the liberation

Name	Transport
Fischel Ludwig	Bielefeld
Fischer Robert	Vienna
Foster Ruth, nee Heilbronn	Bielefeld
Frank Inge, nee Fischel	Bielefeld
Frank Willy	unknown
Franke Elfriede	Bielefeld
Franke Henry (Heinz)	Dortmund
Freiberg Dolly, verw. Spiegel*	Prague
Frenkel Elli	Kassel
Friedjung Franz	Prague
Friedjung, Dr. Hans*	Prague
Friedman Kaethe, nee Zimbler	Berlin
Friedmann Inge, nee Rosenthal	Bielefeld
Friedner Flory, verw. Jacobs-Goldwein	Hanover
Fuerst Gilberg	unknown
Fuerst Helmut	Hanover
Gaffin Genius	unknown
Gans Ernest	Cologne
Gardner Gretel, nee Schaumburger	Duesseldorf
Geissenberger Lothar	Stuttgart
Geissenberger Rose, nee Schubin	Stuttgart
Gerber Irma, nee Salomons	Dortmund
Gersh Mia, nee Safran	Leipzig
Giesskann Georgine	unknown
Ginsburg Liesl, nee Frankel	Duesseldorf
Glas Hans	Dortmund
Glas Lilly, verw. Brodt*	Dortmund
Glaser Egon	Vienna
Glaser Emma, nee Marx	Duesseldorf
Glaser Erwin	Vienna
Glassner Ida	unknown
Gold Dolly, nee Pinkassowitsch	Vienna
Goldberg Karel	unknown

*Died since the liberation

Name	Transport
Goldberg Manfred	unknown
Goldberger Klara	unknown
Goldenberg Else	Bielefeld
Goldenberg Hermann	unknown
Goldenberg Siegfried	Bielefeld
Goldschmidt Walter*	Kassel
Goldschmidt Werner	Dortmund
Goldsmith Berta, verw. Rosenbach	Kassel
Goldsmith Lotte, verw. Hirschhorn	Vienna
Goldstein Claire, nee Franke	Bielefeld
Golin Gregor	unknown
Golin Stella, nee Lewinberg	unknown
Golnik Horst	Kassel
Golnik Irma	Kassel
Golnik Werner	Kassel
Gottschalk Gerda	Leipzig
Gradus Leo	Duesseldorf
Granierer Leah	Vienna
Granierer Leo	Vienna
Greenbaum Regina, nee Litwas	Cologne
Griesbach Marga, nee Steinhardt	unknown
Gross Ruth	Bielefeld
Gruenbaum Bettina, nee Mayer	Cologne
Gruenbaum Manfred	Cologne
Gruenberg Louis	Berlin
Guggenheim Jack (Hans)	Stuttgart
Gutenstein Katie, nee Selling	Nuernberg
Gutherman Rita, nee Speyer	Kassel
Gutman Ludwig	unknown
Haas Ernest	Nuernberg
Haase Bernd	Dortmund
Hacker Renee	unknown
Hahn Marga, nee Loewi	Nuernberg

*Died since the liberation

Name	Transport
Hahn Otto	Nuernberg
Hamburger Berthold*	Hanover
Hammer Selma, nee Hammerschlag	Bielefeld
Harf Emma*	Duesseldorf
Harf Gustav*	Duesseldorf
Harf Meta, nee Seligmann	Duesseldorf
Harf Sigmund	Duesseldorf
Hauser Sally	Vienna
Hausler Hermann	unknown
Heilblut Jakob	unknown
Heilbronn Martha*	Hanover
Heiser Inge, nee Nussbaum	Kassel
Herman Malchen	unknown
Herrmann Bernie*	Cologne
Herrmann Kurt	Cologne
Herrmann Rene	Cologne
Herrmann Rosa	Cologne
Herz Meta, nee Simon	unknown
Herzberg Ilse, nee Feldmann*	Leipzig
Herzog Ceci	Duesseldorf
Hess Harry (Helmut)	Hanover
Hess Herta	unknown
Hess Lona, nee Wolfermann	Hanover
Hess Max	Kassel
Heyman Helen, nee Marx	Duesseldorf
Heymann Else, nee Lion	Duesseldorf
Heymann Hermann	Duesseldorf
Himmelfarb Jehudith	unknown
Hirsch Lisa	Dortmund
Hirsch Max	Dortmund
Hirsch Renee, nee Kraemer	Kassel
Hirschfeld Esther	unknown
Hladka Eliska	unknown
Hochermann Wilhelmina*	Vienna

*Died since the liberation

Name	Transport
Hochheimer Henny*	unknown
Hoffmann Hans-Jochen	Bielefeld
Honigwill Adele	unknown
Horowitz Trudy, nee Guenter	Nuernberg
Hudcova Erna, nee Gluecksmann	Prague
Ilberg Ernst	Leipzig
Illing Horst	Prague
Illing Nelly, nee Stahler	Prague
Ischenhauser Ella	unknown
Isenberg Harry (Hans)	Kassel
Israelson Filia	unknown
Jacobs Guenther	unknown
Jacobs Leo*	Dortmund
Janska Vilda	Prague
Jellinek Fritz	Vienna
Joffe Ruth, nee Katz	Hanover
Jordan Hilde, nee Leeser	Bielefeld
Joseph Sidonie, verw. Hertz	Bielefeld
Joseph Siegfried	unknown
Jurman Ezra	unknown
Kahn Fred	Cologne
Kahn Harry	Stuttgart
Kahn Hilde	unknown
Kahn Jenny, nee Katz	Kassel
Kaliszenki Frieda	unknown
Kallmann Herbert Kurt	Berlin
Kamm Elly, nee Diamont	Dortmund
Kamp Hanna, nee Harf	unknown
Kann Arthur	unknown
Kanter Hugo	Kassel
Kaplan Eliz	Hamburg

*Died since the liberation

Name	Transport
Karten Helen	Duesseldorf
Katz Alfons	unknown
Katz Bernd	Kassel
Katz Daniel	Kassel
Katz Ella*	Kassel
Katz Irene, nee Laermer	Nuernberg
Katz Josef	Hamburg
Katz Joseph	Kassel
Katz Kurt	Kassel
Katz Lothar	unknown
Katz Manfred	Kassel
Katz Mascha	Hamburg
Katz Ruth, nee Rosenbach	Kassel
Katz Selma, nee Kusiel	unknown
Katz Solly (Samuel)	Bielefeld
Katz Siegfried*	Kassel
Kaufman Friedel, nee Levi	Kassel
Kaufman Hilde, nee Lehmann	Hanover
Kaufman Kurt	Cologne
Kaufman Paul	Duesseldorf
Kaufmann Rosa	Nuernberg
Kaufmann Siegfried	unknown
Kimmelstiel Albert	Nuernberg
Kisch Herta, nee Schnitzer	Vienna
Klawanski Irmgard, nee Loewi	Nuernberg
Klainbaum Selma, nee Buchtal	unknown
Klein Hilde	unknown
Kodesch Dora, nee Brueck	Leipzig
Kohn Anna*	Nuernberg
Kohn Julius	Nuernberg
Kollins Susan, nee Sandberg	Kassel
Kornberg Emilie	Hanover
Korycan Cecilie, nee Koritschoner	Prague
Korycan Herman	Prague

*Died since the liberation

Name	Transport
Kraemer Walter	Kassel
Kratochvil Marie (Mici Roth)	Prague
Krongelb Helga, nee Levi	Dortmund
Kugelmann Lina*	Kassel
Kummermann Marta	unknown
Kuerth Hertha	Vienna
Kuttenplan Ruth*	Vienna
Labaton Anni, nee Steuer	Hanover
Lachman Walter (Wolfgang)	Berlin
Lakeman Ilse, nee Kornberg	Hanover
Lamac Otto	unknown
Landau Antek	unknown
Landes Margot, nee Kogan	Leipzig
Lang Albert	Vienna
Lang Kurt	Stuttgart
Lang Trude, nee Oser	Vienna
Lang Siegfried	Stuttgart
Langer Hanna, nee Fessler	Prague
Lankisch-Hoernitz Arthur (von)	Prague
Laster Mathilde	Vienna
Lawton (Levinson) Kuxi	Berlin
Lawton Lotte, nee Berger	Duesseldorf
Lazarus Irmgard, nee Speier	Kassel
Lehman Clotilde, nee Lindo	Nuernberg
Lehman Gerda, nee Leeser	Duesseldorf
Lehman Marianne, nee Buchheim	Bielefeld
Leib Max	unknown
Lemberger Ruth, nee Lang	Stuttgart
Lemberger Sol	Stuttgart
Leopold Lotte, verw. Nussbaum	Dortmund
Leston Sofie, verw. Rothschild	Kassel
Levi Egon*	Stuttgart
Levi Julius	Kassel

*Died since the liberation

Name	Transport
Levi Walter*	Duesseldorf
Levie Erna	Dortmund
Levie Erwin*	Dortmund
Levine Elsa, nee Holzer	Vienna
Levy Alfred*	Hanover
Levy Bertha	Stuttgart
Levy Harold (Hans)	Hanover
Levy Henny, nee Gradus	Duesseldorf
Levy Joseph (Jupp)	Cologne
Levy Paula, nee Rappaport*	Hanover
Levy Selma, nee Kanter	Kassel
Lind Eric	unknown
Lipton Sonia, nee Habler	Kassel
Loheit Victor	unknown
Loewenstein Emmi, nee Nathan	Duesseldorf
Loewi Rosa	Nuernberg
Loszynski Hans Werner	Hamburg
Lowenberg Martin	Kassel
Lowengrad Edith	unknown
Lowenstein Ellen, verw. Laumann	Bielefeld
Lowenstein Dr. Margot	unknown
Lucas Henry (Horst)*	Duesseldorf
Lustbader Ingrid, nee Rosenstein	Kassel
Lutumen Lotte, nee Ostertag	Hanover
Machlin Netty, nee Hecht	Dortmund
Mai Herbert	Nuernberg
Mandelberger Leo	unknown
Mann Joseph	Duesseldorf
Manne Erika	Hanover
Manne Martin	Hanover
Mannheimer Lina	Kassel
Marcusfeld Lore, nee Duehring	Hamburg
Markiewicz Henny, nee Rosenbaum	Hanover

*Died since the liberation

Name	Transport
Marx Alice, nee Ganzweiler	Duesseldorf
Marx Edith, nee Wolff	Dortmund
Marx Emmi	unknown
Marx Frieda	Cologne
Marx Hannelore, nee Kahn	Stuttgart
Marx Hannelore, nee Simons	Dortmund
Marx Jacob*	Cologne
Marx Victor	Stuttgart
Maurueber Tilly	Vienna
Mausner Vera, nee Kisch	Vienna
Mayer Edith, verw. Steinberg-Hess	Hanover
Mayer Irene	unknown
Mayer Max	unknown
Mayer Ruth, nee Gans	Cologne
Menczel Lili, nee Simons	Cologne
Mendel Emmi, nee Dahl	Duesseldorf
Mendel Kurt	Duesseldorf
Metzger Ernst	Dortmund
Metzger Eva	Dortmund
Metzger Kurt	unknown
Metzger Max	Dortmund
Meyer Alice, nee Gundersheim	Nuernberg
Mirkin Ilse, nee Goldschmidt	Kassel
Mittel Inge, nee Benjamin	Dortmund
Montrose Deborah, nee Ferche	Hanover
Mosbach Erwin	Hanover
Moschewitz Selma, nee Wollenstein	Hanover
Mudrsik Jindra	Prague
Mueller Elfriede, nee Rerucha	Vienna
Nathan Sophie	Duesseldorf
Nathan Thea	Duesseldorf
Nebel Ruth, nee Stern	Hamburg
Nelson Hannelore	unknown

*Died since the liberation

Name	Transport
Nettl Hans	unknown
Nettler Werner Georg	Berlin
Neu Jacob	unknown
Neudorf Bella, nee Silbermann	Nuernberg
Neudorf Hermann	Bielefeld
Neumann Leona	Vienna
Neumann Rudolf	Vienna
Neuwald Anni	unknown
Neuwald Kurt	Dortmund
Niselewitz Marga, nee Oppenheimer*	Kassel
Nistler Helene*	Vienna
Noerdlinger Alfred	Stuttgart
Noveck Meta, nee Meyer	Stuttgart
Nussbaum Fritz*	Dortmund
Nyman Ruth, nee Kleestadt	Hanover
Oppenheim Vera	Hanover
Oppenheimer Erika, nee Mannheimer	Kassel
Oppenheimer Julius	Kassel
Oppenheimer Leo	Kassel
Oppenheimer Lore, nee Pels	Hanover
Oppenheimer Margie, nee Hoffmann	Bielefeld
Oschrin Rosel, nee Affenkraut	Leipzig
Pancis Lilli, nee Fischel	Bielefeld
Pasch Grete	Prague
Pasch Susie	Prague
Pergamenter Walter	unknown
Pick Larry (Lutz)	Prague
Pick Regina, verw. Schwartz	Vienna
Pinkassowitsch Erich*	Vienna
Pisk Erich	Vienna
Polak Ilse	Bielefeld
Pollack Charlotte, nee Friedler	Dortmund

*Died since the liberation

Name	Transport
Popper Hanka*	Prague
Popperova Olga	Prague
Posament Otto*	Vienna
Posament Steffi, nee Schybilski	Berlin
Prayer Mela	unknown
Rabinowitz Frieda, nee Meyer	Stuttgart
Rabinowitz Julia	unknown
Rackova Irena, nee Popper	Prague
Radin Ruth, nee Weinberg	Bielefeld
Railes Margot	Hamburg
Rails Margot	Nuernberg
Rappaport Adolf	unknown
Rassen Jacob	unknown
Rath Hannah, nee Lenschitzki	Hanover
Reichenthal Carla, nee Pins*	Bielefeld
Reingenheim Selma	Bielefeld
Reiniger Malvina*	Prague
Reisler Berta	unknown
Reissner Harold	Nuernberg
Ritchie Lydia, nee Reichmann	Vienna
Rosas Heini	Stuttgart
Rosas Lisl, nee Rosenrauch-Wolf	Stuttgart
Roseboom Kurt	Berlin
Roseboom Ruth, nee Willner	Cologne
Rosen Frieda	Duesseldorf
Rosenblum Selma, verw. Sollinger	Hanover
Rosenfeld Irma	Bielefeld
Rosenhein Caeci, nee Stern	Hanover
Rosenhein Heini	Hanover
Rosengarten Julius*	Kassel
Rosenkrantz Felicia	Vienna
Rosenstein Howard	Kassel
Rosenthal Heinz	Berlin

*Died since the liberation

Name	Transport
Rosenthal Johanna	Berlin
Ross Renee, verw. Kohn	Hanover
Rotfeld Anna	Vienna
Rotfeld Inge	Vienna
Roth Gusti	Vienna
Rothschild Phillip	Cologne
Rothschild Werner	Kassel
Rothstein Hanna	Hanover
Rotmueller-Wiener Mathilde	Vienna
Rowen (Rosenstern) Ernest	Hanover
Rozman Ilse, nee Kaufmann	Cologne
Rubinger Anni, nee Reisler	Dortmund
Rubinstein Regina, nee Belensky	Leipzig
Ruebsteck Ilse, nee Falkenstein	unknown
Ruebsteck Kurt	unknown
Ruf Manfred	Cologne
Sachs Arthur	Bielefeld
Sachs Berta	Bielefeld
Safran Golda	Leipzig
Saguta Fanny, nee Ostrowski	Leipzig
Salomon Ruth, nee Franke	Bielefeld
Salomons Hertha*	Dortmund
Samuel Heinz	Duesseldorf
Samuel Margot, nee Frankenstein	Duesseldorf
Samuel Ruth, nee Gompertz	Duesseldorf
Samuel Werner	Duesseldorf
Sauer Ilse, nee Rudolphson	Berlin
Schick Irena, nee Popper	Prague
Schick Dr. Jindra	Prague
Schiff Berthold*	Kassel
Schloss Eric	Nuernberg
Schloss Lewis (Lutz)	Dortmund
Schloss Liesel, nee Levi-Froehlich	Nuernberg

*Died since the liberation

Name	Transport
Schloss Trudy, nee Ullmann	Stuttgart
Schmertz Hilde, nee Nolting	Cologne
Schmitz Walter	Cologne
Schneebalg Lina, nee Stern	Nuernberg
Schneider Dr. Gertrude (Traudl), nee Hirschhorn	Vienna
Schneider Helma, nee Baruch	Cologne
Schneider Karl*	Cologne
Schneller Edith	Vienna
Schreiber Beate, nee Rosenbach	Kassel
Schreiber Simon	Kassel
Schuerenberg Kurt	unknown
Schultz Herbert	Cologne
Schusheim Hanna Liese, nee Freudenthal	Cologne
Schuster Margot, nee Schild	Cologne
Schwartz Bertl	Stuttgart
Schwartzman Inge, nee Stern	Bielefeld
Schwarz Else	Cologne
Schwarz Herbert	Vienna
Schybilski Rose*	Berlin
Scott Agnes Lotte, verw. Scheucher	Berlin
Seger Anna	unknown
Seger Josef	unknown
Sekules Else	Vienna
Sekules Erwin	Vienna
Seligson Lore, nee Fischel	Bielefeld
Selling Ignatz	Nuernberg
Sender Marga, nee Goldwein	Kassel
Senger Harry	Berlin
Servos Kurt	Duesseldorf
Sherman Hilde, nee Winter	Duesseldorf
Silber Karla, nee Wollenstein	Hanover
Simberg Rosa*	Bielefeld
Simon Herbert	Hamburg
Simon Rosa, nee Loeser	Duesseldorf

*Died since the liberation

Name	Transport
Simon Hilde, nee Loeb	Hamburg
Simons Helmut	Cologne
Simons Sally	Cologne
Sindelar Hermine	unknown
Sklan Vera, nee Weinstein	Berlin
Skura Lotte, nee Kaufmann	Duesseldorf
Skurnik Paula, nee Goldstein	Vienna
Solms Teddy	Nuernberg
Sonn Bettina, nee Halle	Nuernberg
Sonnenberg Gertrud, nee Michelsohn	Hanover
Sonnenschein Ernst	Vienna
Spangenthal Kurt	Kassel
Speier Hermann*	Kassel
Speier Julius*	Bielefeld
Speier Margret	Bielefeld
Spiegel Herta, verw. Pels	Hanover
Springfield Rita, nee Kaplan	Hamburg
Stastny Felix	unknown
Steier Luisa	unknown
Stein Bedrich	unknown
Stein Fanny	unknown
Steinbach Kurt	Vienna
Steinhardt Therese	Kassel
Steinmetz Edith	Stuttgart
Steinweg Edith, nee Stahler	Prague
Steinweg Ernst	Bielefeld
Steinweg Kurt	Duesseldorf
Steinweg Walter	Duesseldorf
Stern Edith, nee Rosen	Duesseldorf
Stern Erna	Kassel
Stern Henry (Heinz)	Bielefeld
Stern Karl	Kassel
Stern Markus*	Bielefeld
Stern Margot, nee Wertheimer	Stuttgart

*Died since the liberation

Name	Transport
Stern Minna, nee Buxbaum	Kassel
Stern Peter	Nuernberg
Stern Siegfried	Kassel
Sternberg Harry (Heinz)*	Duesseldorf
Stone (Rudziejewski) Rolf	Nuernberg
Strand Hannelore, nee Ziedower	Hanover
Strauss Bert Lutz	Kassel
Strauss Israel Guenther	Kassel
Strauss Joseph*	Kassel
Strauss Lilly	Kassel
Strauss Margie (Putti), nee Israel	Hanover
Streicher Rosa, nee Goldapper	Vienna
Sturm Herbert	Nuernberg
Suesskind Benno*	Cologne
Sugar Margrit, nee Samson	unknown
Suss Fritz	Prague
Suss Martha, nee Stahler	Prague
Sussking Minna, nee Cohn	unknown
Taube Susan, nee Strauss	Berlin
Temel Hannelore (Hanka), nee Spiegel	Prague
Temersohn Judith	Berlin
Tepper Max	Dortmund
Terhoch Herta, nee Sachs	unknown
Theisebach Walter	Duesseldorf
Translateur Helma, nee Kaufmann	Duesseldorf
Trost Frieda	Vienna
Tycho Oskar	Vienna
Ullmann Gustav*	Bielefeld
Ullmann Irwin	Stuttgart
Ullmann Max	Stuttgart
Urbach Kurt	Vienna

*Died since the liberation

Name	Transport
Valk Erna	Duesseldorf
Valk Walter*	Duesseldorf
Van Dyck Nina, nee von Sonnenthal	Vienna
Vorel Jiri	Prague
Voos Dagobert*	Cologne
Vosen Flora	Dortmund
Vosen Hermann	Dortmund
Wachtel Max	unknown
Waldhorn Elli	Bielefeld
Wallhausen Guenther	Bielefeld
Wasserberger Ruth, nee Brumsak	Hanover
Wasserman David	unknown
Wasserman Erich	Nuernberg
Wasserman Gerda, nee Rose	Hamburg
Wassermann Rita, nee Hirschhorn	Vienna
Weil Selma	Stuttgart
Weiler Horst	unknown
Weinberg Arthur	Kassel
Weinberg Erich	Bielefeld
Weinberg Siegfried	Bielefeld
Weingel Lea, nee Hirschfeld	unknown
Weinheber Elena	Vienna
Weinstein Grete	unknown
Weintraub Lore, nee Simberg	Berlin
Weiss Elizabeth	Vienna
Weissenstein Otto	Vienna
Weisskopf Lia	Vienna
Welles Elliot	Vienna
Weltman Ilse, nee Bardos	Prague
Wernick Edith, nee Marchand	unknown
Westermann Alexander	unknown
Wettenstein Minna, nee Gruber	Vienna
Willner Betty, nee Rothschild	Nuernberg

*Died since the liberation

Name	Transport
Willner Ludwig	Nuernberg
Wilzig Erwin	Berlin
Windmueller Otto	unknown
Winkler Selma	unknown
Winter Alfred	Duesseldorf
Winter Franz	unknown
Winter Herbert	Duesseldorf
Winternitz Elizabeth*	Vienna
Wodak Alfred	Prague
Wolf Alice, nee Weil	Stuttgart
Wolf Carrie, nee Sichel	Nuernberg
Wolf Emil	unknown
Wolferman Ruth	Hanover
Wolff Hanna, nee Braun	Cologne
Wolff Henni, nee Franke	Bielefeld
Wolff Jeanette	Dortmund
Wolff Max	Cologne
Wolfinger Fritzi, nee Kohn	Vienna
Wollenberger Eva	unknown
Wulf Harry	unknown
Yashek Richard	unknown
Zajouc Lilly, nee Stahler	Prague
Zeilberger Fred	Nuernberg
Zeiss Margot, nee Jacobs	Dortmund
Zetley Grete, nee Hammerschlag	Bielefeld
Ziedover Hannelore	Hanover
Ziegler Jonni	Hanover
Ziering Cilly	Kassel
Ziering Hermann	Kassel
Ziering, Dr. Sigi	Kassel
Zinner Alice	Vienna
Zinner Edith	Vienna

*Died since the liberation

C
Documents

Secret Letter Written by Lange to Heinrich Lohse
in Regard to Jewish Transports

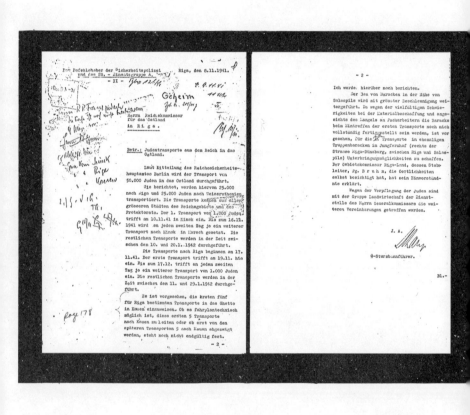

Commander of the Security Police & Riga,
Security Service, Einsatzgruppe A Nov. 8, 1941

SECRET

To: Reichskommissar for the Ostland

Re: Jewish transports from the Reich to the Ostland

As per the information received from the Reichssicherheitshaupt-amt, 50,000 Jews will be shipped to the East.

As reported, 25,000 will be shipped to Riga and 25,000 to White Ruthenia. The transports come from all larger cities of the Reich and the Protectorat. The first contingent of 1,000 Jews will arrive in Minsk on November 10, 1941. Until the 16 December 1941, the transports will arrive at the rate of one every two days. The remaining transports will be sent during the time from January 10 to January 20, 1942.

Transports to Riga will begin on November 17, 1941, with the first contingent arriving here on the 19th. Until December 17, there will be further contingents of 1,000 Jews each arriving every second day. The remaining transports will be sent between January 11 and 29, 1942.

There are plans to send the first five transports meant for Riga to the Ghetto in Kovno instead. If it is technically possible to do this with the first five, or with later ones, has not been decided definitely. I will let you know about it.

Barracks are being built near Salaspils as fast as possible. Since there are difficulties in obtaining materials and also due to a lack of experts, the barracks will not be finished when the first contingents arrive. It is therefore planned to house them in the former troop barracks of Jung-fernhof (Jumpramuize), to the right of the Riga-Duenaburg Road, be-tween Riga and Salaspils.

The commissar of the area Riga-Land agreed. His staff-leader, Member of the Party Bruhn, went to see the places himself.

As far as food for the Jews is concerned, arrangements were made with the office of the Generalkommissar and with the Farm Adminis-tration.

Signed Dr. Lange

Telegram Implementing the Final Solution
of Jewish Transports in Latvia

```
Fernschreibstelle     HRAX  1316
[  |  |  ]
Fernschreibnamen  Laufende Nummer

++++ HRZ 97759  13. 11. 41 1745===

AN DEN HERRN REICHSKOMMISSAR FUER DAS OSTLAND, RIGA ==

-- BETR.:-- TELEGRAMM V. 9. 11. 41 .-       Bestimmungsort

- BEZUEGLICH JUDENTRANSPORTE IN DAS OSTLAND.-

GENAUES SCHREIBEN UNTERWEGS . JUDEN KOMMEN WEITER NACH OSTEN

LAGER IN RIGA UND MINSK NUR VORLAEUFIG E MASSNAHME /DAHER HIE

KEINE BEDENKEN ====


DR. LEITBRANDT, REICHSMINISTERIUM FUER DIE BESETZTEN
                                      OSTGEBIETE ++


++++0205 EINS LU HRAX ++
```

Telegram

November 13, 1941

To the Reichskommissar for the Ostland

In regard to Jewish transports to the Ostland.
Exact information is on the way.
Jews will go further east.
Camps in Riga and Minsk only temporary measures, therefore no doubts here.

Signed: Dr. Leibbrandt, Reichsministry of the occupied territories

Note on the bottom of telegram, signed "L" as Lange did:

Get in touch with Obergruppenfuehrer Jeckel.
Transit camps to be moved further east, if possible.

November 16

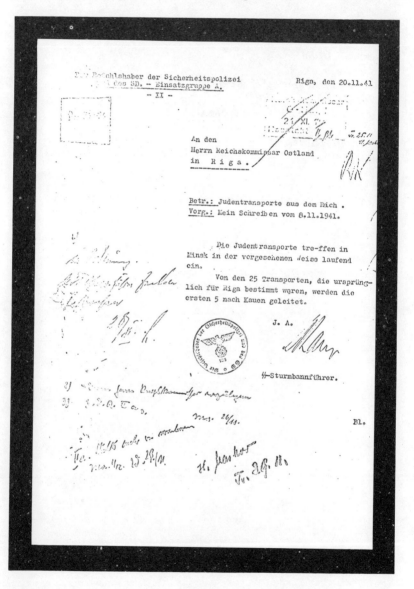

Der Befehlshaber der Sicherheitspolizei
und des SD. – Einsatzgruppe A.
– II –

Riga, den 20.11.41

An den
Herrn Reichskommissar Ostland
in R i g a .

Betr.: Judentransporte aus dem Reich .
Vorg.: Mein Schreiben vom 8.11.1941.

Die Judentransporte treffen in
Minsk in der vorgesehenen Weise laufend
ein.

Von den 25 Transporten, die ursprünglich für Riga bestimmt waren, werden die
ersten 5 nach Kauen geleitet.

J. A.

SS-Sturmbannführer.

Bl.

Commander of the Security Police &   Riga,
Security Service, Einsatzgruppe A   November 20, 1941

To: Reichskommissar for the Ostland

Re: Jewish transports from the Reich, my letter of November 8, 1941.

The Jewish transports will arrive in Minsk as planned. Of the twenty-five transports originally meant for Riga, the first five will be sent to Kovno.

Signed Dr. Lange

Letter Reflecting Confusion in the Various Plans
for Jewish Transports from the Reich

Der Reichsminister
für die besetzten Ostgebiete

Berlin W.35, den 4. Dezember 1941
Rauchstraße 17/18
Fernsprecher: 21 95 15 und 39 89 45
Drahtanschrift: Reichsministerost

Nr. I/293/41

Tgb. Nr. 345/41 g

An den
Herrn Reichskommissar für das Ostland

R i g a
Leitort Tilsit

Betr.: Lösung der Judenfrage.

Mir sind die dortigen Vorgänge des Herrn Generalkommissars
in Riga bezüglich des Transportes von Juden aus dem Alt-
reich nach Riga sowie die Errichtung von Judenlagern
zugeleitet worden. Wie SS-Obergruppenführer H e y d r i c h
bei einer Besprechung vor wenigen Tagen mitteilte, soll
das Judenlager, dessen Errichtung in der Umgebung von
Riga geplant war, in die Gegend von Pleskau kommen. Ich
habe bereits mit Schreiben vom 13. 11. 1941 das Reichssicherheitshauptamt gebeten, mich in Zukunft vor Einlei-
tung von Maßnahmen zur Durchführung der Lösung der Judenfrage zu unterrichten, damit die Schwierigkeiten, die
bisher durch die mangelnde oder zu späte Inkenntnissetzung
meiner Stellen entstanden sind, vermieden werden.

Im Auftrag

(gez.) Leibbrandt
Beglaubigt

Regierungsinspektor

The Reichsminister
for the occupied territories

Berlin
December 4, 1941

To: The Reichskommissar for the Ostland
Riga via Tilsit

Re: Solution of the Jewish Question

I was informed about the actions of the Generalkommissar in Riga in regard to the transports of Jews from the Reich, as well as to the erection of camps for Jews. Several days ago, at a meeting, SS Obergruppenfuehrer Heydrich announced that the camp for Jews, which was planned to be in the environs of Riga, would be erected in the vicinity of Pleskau (Pskov) instead. On November 13 I wrote to the Reichssicherheitshauptamt, asking to be informed in the future before measures are contemplated, so that the difficulties arising from letting me know too little or too late can be avoided.

Signed: Leibbrandt

Letter Reflecting the Squabbles between Administrative Offices over the Handling of Jews and Their Valuables

Riga, den 11. Dezember 41.

1.) Die Herren Drech und Schulz machten mir Mitteilung davon, dass 4000 Juden aus dem Reich hier angekommen seien und dass Cur CO beabsichtigt, diese Juden in den Rigaer Ghetto unterzubringen. Herr Altemeyer der hierzu gehört wurde, erklärte es sei unmöglich die Verantwortung für die Vermögensgegenstände, die noch im Ghetto liegen, wenn nunmehr wiederum neue Juden in das Ghetto gelegt werden und damit eine dritte interessierte Stelle Eingang in das Ghetto gewinne:

Herr Altemeyer setzte sich mit dem Sturmbannführer Dr. Lange ins Benehmen und wird über das Ergebnis seines Gespräches einen Aktenvermerk einreichen.

2.) Gestern abend hatte ich Gelegenheit mit dem SS Sturmbannführer Dr. Lange zu unterhalten und über die Frage der Belegung des Ghettos durch deutsche Juden zu sprechen. Herr Dr. Lange er hierzu mit, dass in die ... 20000 Juden aus dem Reich zu rechnen sei und dass er bitte diese Juden in das Ghetto aufzunehmen. Ich erklärte ihm, dass es mir nicht möglich sei die Juden aufzunehmen, zumal die Vermögensgegenstände der inzwischen umgesiedelten Juden noch nicht hätten erfasst werden können.

Der Reichskommissar habe erklärt, dass die Verantwortung für die Durchführung der Beschlagnahme des jüdischen Vermögens nach wie vor den Gebietskommissar obliege.

Unter diesen Umständen müsse ich bis zur völligen Sicherstellung der jüdischen Vermögensgegenstände, die Übernahme neuer Juden ins Ghetto untersagen.

Dr. Lange erklärte mir demgegenüber, dass er bereits 2000 Juden in das Ghetto hereingebracht habe und dass diese in einigen Coz... der ... gebracht seien.

Ich erklärte gegen, dass dies dann ohne Verwissen und Genehmigung des Gebietskommissars erfolgt sei und dass ich daher ihm den Sturmbannführer Dr. Lange - die Verantwortung für die jüdischen Vermögensgegenstände zuschieben müsse, es sei mir durch sein Handlungsweise unmöglich gemacht ... die Sicherung des jüdischen Vermögens sicherzustellen.

Riga, December 11, 1941

1) Mr. Brasch and Mr. Schulz informed me that 4,000 Jews from the Reich have arrived here and that it is the intent of the Security Service to house them in the ghetto of Riga. According to Mr. Altemeyer, it is impossible to be responsible for objects of value still in the ghetto, if new Jews were to be brought there, since a third party would thus have access to the ghetto. Mr. Altemeyer contacted Sturmbannfuehrer Dr. Lange, and is to report on the result of their discussion.

2) Last night I had the opportunity to talk with Dr. Lange about the question of German Jews being housed in the ghetto. Dr. Lange explained to me that we could count on receiving another 10,000 from the Reich within a short time; he asked that they be accepted into the ghetto. I explained to him that it would be impossible for me to take these Jews in, since we had not as yet been able to take out the valuables left there by those Jews who had in the meantime been resettled.

Since the Reichskommissar had declared that the responsibility for the collection of Jewish wealth still belonged to the area's commissar, I would have to prevent the housing of new Jews in the ghetto until I could secure the Jewish objects of wealth still there.

Dr. Lange explained, however, that he had already brought 1,000 Jews to the ghetto and that they were quartered in several houses.

I, on the other hand, explained that this had been done without the knowledge or permission of the area's commissar and that I would make Sturmbannfuehrer Dr. Lange responsible for the Jewish valuables. Because of his action I would be unable to secure the items.

Dr. Lange then said that during the absence of the Reichskommissar the Higher SS and Police Leader was his substitute and that an order to that effect was contained in a secret edict, sent out a week earlier. I said that I had never heard of such an edict, and asked to be sent

this in writing, so that I could be relieved of all responsibility vis-a-vis the Reichskommissar. I also said that I would send in a written complaint to make my position clear. Dr. Lange in turn promised to answer my letter immediately.

3) Letter sent to Higher SS and Police, attention Dr. Lange.

4) Notice presented December 13, 1941.

Letter Insisting that Economic Considerations are to be Ignored in the Final Solution

3666-PS

Der Reichsminister
für die besetzten Ostgebiete

Berlin W 35, den 18.Dezember 1941
Rauchstraße 17/18
Fernsprecher: 21 95 15 und 39 59 65
Drahtanschrift: Reichsminister

Nr. I/1/157/41 geh.Reichssache

Geheime Reichssache

An den
Herrn Reichskommissar für das Ostland

R i g a / Leitort Tilsit
Adolf Hitler Strasse

Betrifft: Judenfrage
Auf das Schreiben vom 15,11.1941

In der Judenfrage dürfte inzwischen durch mündliche
Besprechungen Klarheit geschaffen sein. Wirtschaftliche
Belange sollen bei der Regelung des Problems grundsätz-
lich unberücksichtigt bleiben. Im übrigen wird gebeten,
auftauchende Fragen unmittelbar mit dem höheren SS - und
Polizeiführer zu regeln.

Im Auftrag

"ATTACHMENT C"

A 097128

The Reichsminister
for the occupied territories

Berlin
December 18, 1941

SECRET MATTER OF STATE

To the Reichskommissar for the Ostland
  Riga via Tilsit

Re: Jewish Question
  Letter of November 15, 1941.

As per our conversations, matters concerning the Jewish Question should be cleared up by now. When solving the problem, economic considerations are to be ignored. It is asked, furthermore, to settle any future questions with the higher SS and police leader.

Signed Braeutigam

A Letter Indicating the Need for Skilled Jewish Labor

Der Reichskommissar
für das Ostland

Riga, den , Dezember 1941

Abt.: II a Tgb.Nr.220/41 g.

An
den Reichskommissar f.d.Ostland
- Höherer SS- und Polizeiführer -

in R i g a

die Herren Generalkommissare
in R e v a l
R i g a
K a u e n
M i n s k

Nachrichtlich an den Wehrmachtbefehlshaber Ostland

in R i g a

Der Chefintendant beim Wehrmachtbefehlshaber Ostland
beschwert sich darüber, dass der Wehrmacht in Rüstungsbetrieb
und Reparaturwerkstätten jüdische Facharbeiter durch Liquidation entzogen würden, die dort zur Zeit nicht zu ersetzen
sind.

Ich ersuche nachdrücklichst die Liquidation von Juden zu
verhindern, die in Rüstungsbetrieben und Reparaturwerkstätten der Wehrmacht als Fachkräfte tätig und zur Zeit durch
Einheimische nicht zu ersetzen sind. Das Einvernehmen darüber
wer zu den unersetzlichen jüdischen Arbeitskräften gehört,
ist mit den Gebietskommissaren (Abtlg. Soziale Verwaltung)
zu erzielen.

Für Schulung geeigneten einheimischen Nachwuchses als
Facharbeiter ist beschleunigt Sorge zu tragen.

Das gleiche gilt für jüdische Fachkräfte in Betrieben,
die nicht unmittelbar den Zwecken der Wehrmacht dienen, aber
wichtige Aufgaben im Rahmen der Kriegswirtschaft zu erfüllen
haben.

"ATTACHMENT B-2"

192

The Reichskommissar for   Riga, December 1941
the Ostland

To: Reichskommissar for the Ostland - higher SS and Police leader in Riga

To: The General commissars in Reval, Riga, Kovno, Minsk
Copy to the Army High Command Ostland in Riga

The official in charge at the Army High Command Ostland has complained that due to liquidation skilled Jewish workers had been removed from army munition factories as well as repair parks. They are irreplaceable at this time.

I seriously urge you to prevent the liquidation of such skilled Jews working in the army's munition factories and repair parks, since they cannot, at this time, be replaced by natives. As to who is irreplaceable should be discussed and agreed upon with the areas' commissars of the Department for Social Organization.

Natives who can be taught, are to be trained as quickly as possible.

The above guidelines are to be applied also to those skilled Jewish workers who are not exactly serving the army, but are equally important in regard to wartime economy.

Düsseldorf, den 26. Dezember 1941

V e r t r a u l i c h !

B e r i c h t

über die Evakuierung von Juden nach Riga.

Transportbegleitung in Stärke von 1/15

vom 11.12. - 17.12. 1941.

1.) Transportverlauf.

Der für den 11.12. 1941 vorgesehene Judentransport umfasste 1007
Juden aus den Städten Duisburg, Krefeld, mehreren kleineren
Städten und Landgemeinden des rhein.westf. Industriegebietes.
Düsseldorf war nur mit 19 Juden vertreten. Der Transport setzte
sich aus Juden beiderlei Geschlechts und verschiedenen Alters, vom
Säugling bis zum Alter von 65 Jahren, zusammen.
Die Ablassung des Transportes war für 9,30 Uhr vorgesehen, weshalb
die Juden bereits ab 4 Uhr an der Verladerampe zur Verladung be-
reitgestellt waren. Die Reichsbahn konnte jedoch den Sonderzug,
angeblich wegen Personalmangels, nicht so früh zusammenstellen, so dass
mit der Einladung der Juden erst gegen 9 Uhr begonnen werden konnte.
Das Einladen wurde, da die Reichsbahn auf eine möglichst fahr-
planmässige Ablassung des Zuges drängte, mit der grössten Hast
vorgenommen. Es war daher nicht verwunderlich, dass einzelne Wagen
überladen waren (60 - 65 Personen), während andere nur mit 35 -
40 Personen besetzt waren. Dieser Umstand hat sich während des
ganzen Transportes bis Riga nachteilig ausgewirkt, da einzelne
Juden immer wieder versuchten, in weniger stark besetzte Wagen
zu gelangen. Soweit Zeit zur Verfügung stand, habe ich dann auch in
einigen Fällen, weil auch Mütter von ihren Kindern getrennt worden
waren, Umlegungen vorgenommen.
Auf dem Wege vom Schlachthof zur Verladerampe hatte ein männlicher
Jude versucht, Selbstmord durch Überfahren mittels der Strassenbahn zu verüben. Er wurde jedoch von der Auffangvorrichtung der
Strassenbahn erfasst und nur leichter verletzt. Er stellte sich
anfänglich sterbend, wurde aber während der Fahrt bald sehr munter,
als er merkte, dass er dem Schicksal der Evakuierung nicht entgehen
konnte. Ebenfalls hatte sich eine ältere Jüdin unbemerkt von der
Verladerampe, es regnete und war sehr dunkel, entfernt, sich in
ein nahe liegendes Haus geflüchtet, entkleidet und auf ein Klosett
gesetzt. Eine Putzfrau hatte sie jedoch bemerkt, so dass auch sie
dem Transport wieder zugeführt werden konnte.
Die Verladung der Juden war gegen 10,15 Uhr beendet. Nach mehr-
maligem Rangieren verliess der Zug dann gegen 10,30 Uhr den Güter-
bahnhof Düsseldorf-Derendorf in Richtung Wuppertal, also schon

-2-

- 2 -

mit einer Verspätung von einer Stunde. Nach dem letzten Rangieren
in Düsseldorf stellte ich fest, dass der Wagen des Begleitkommandos
(2.Klasse), anstatt in die Mitte des Zuges, am Ende der Personen-
wagen, also als 21. Wagen einrangiert worden war. Hinter unserem
Wagen befanden sich dann die 7 mit Gepäck beladenen Güterwagen. Die
falsche Einrangierung des Begleitwagens hatte folgende Nachteile:

   a) Der Dampfdruck erreichte infolge fehlerhafter Heizungsanlagen
      die hinteren Wagen nicht. Infolge der Kälte konnte die Kleidung
      der Posten nicht trocknen (fast während des ganzen Transportes
      regnete es), so dass ich mit Ausfällen durch Erkrankung zu
      rechnen hatte.

   b) Dem Transportführer ging die Übersicht über den Zug ver-
      loren. Wenn auch die mitgeführten Scheinwerfer gute Dienste
      leisteten, so hatten die Posten bei jedem Halten einen zu
      weiten Weg zur Aufsicht über die ersten Wagen zurückzulegen
      und oft Mühe, bei plötzlicher Abfahrt des Zuges noch den
      Wagen des Begleitkommandos zu erreichen. Ausserdem versuchte
      die Juden immer wieder, sofort nach dem Halten in Bahnhof-
      hallen mit dem reisenden Publikum in Verbindung zu treten.
      Post abzugeben oder sich Wasser holen zu lassen. Ich musste
      mich daher entschliessen, 2 Posten in einem Abteil des vor-
      deren Personenwagens unterzubringen.
      Meine diesbezüglichen Einwendungen auf dem Abgangsbahnhof
      Düsseldorf blieben unberücksichtigt und der Zug wurde mit
      dem Bemerken abgelassen, dass infolge der Verspätung in
      Düsseldorf eine Umrangierung des Wagens des Begleitkommandos
      nicht mehr erfolgen könne. Die Umrangierung des Wagens
      könne auch unterwegs erfolgen.

Die Fahrt verlief dann planmässig und berührte folgende Städte:
Wuppertal, Hagen, Schwerte, Hamm. Gegen 18 Uhr wurde Hannover-
Linden erreicht. Hier hatte der Zug einen Aufenthalt von fast
einer Stunde. Ich liess einem Teil der Juden etwas Wasser verabfolgen
und erbat gleichzeitig die Umrangierung des Wagens. Eine Zusage
wurde mir gegeben, jedoch war in letzter Minute keine Rangierlok.
vorhanden. Der Bahnhof in Stendal sollte jedoch entsprechende Nachricht erhalten, damit meinem Wunsche dort entsprochen werden
konnte. Die Fahrt führte dann bis zur Station Misterhorst. Hier
wurde um 21 Uhr ein Achsenbrand am Wagen 12 festgestellt. Der
Wagen musste ausrangiert und die Juden dieses Wagens, weil die
Station keinen Ersatzwagen stellen konnte, auf andere Wagen ver-
teilt werden. Diese Aktion schien den schlafenden Juden durchaus
nicht zu passen und gestaltete sich wegen unaufhörlichen Regens
und Dunkelheit sowie mit Rücksicht darauf, dass der Zug ausser-
halb des Bahnhofs ohne Bahnsteig stand, anfänglich etwas schwierig,
wurde aber mit entsprechendem Nachdruck dennoch sehr schnell
durchgeführt. Bei der Umladung haben sich die mitgeführten Schein-
werfer sehr gut bewährt. Der Bahnhof Stendal wurde um 23 Uhr

-3-

Duesseldorf, December 26, 1941

Secret Report
concerning the evacuation of Jews to Riga, Dec. 11 to Dec. 17

Transport Escort 1/15

1) Events occurring during the transport

The convoy of Jews scheduled for Dec. 11, 1941, consisted of 1,007
Jews from the cities of Duisburg, Krefeld, and several small towns and
villages from the Rhein-Westfalen industrial sections. There were only
19 Jews from Duesseldorf. They were of both sexes and ranged in age
from infant to 65 years. The transport had been scheduled to leave at
9:30 A.M. and for this reason, the Jews were ordered to the loading
ramp for 4:00 A.M. However, the railroad could not prepare the
special train that early—ostensibly because of a lack of personnel—and
therefore the actual loading of the Jews was first started at 9:00. Since
the railroad urged the departure of the train in accordance with its
original schedule, the loading was done in great haste. No wonder then,
that some cars were overloaded, containing between 60 and 65 persons,
while others only contained 35 to 40 persons. Because of this, throughout the trip to Riga, there were always some Jews who tried to get into
these "emptier" cars. In some cases, provided there was time, I made
such transfers myself, especially since some mothers had been separated
from their children.

On the way from the slaughterhouse* to the loading ramp, a male Jew
tried to commit suicide by throwing himself in front of a tram. He was
caught by the specially constructed front bumper of the tram and
sustained only slight injuries. At first he pretended to be near death,
but when he realized that he could not escape the fate of his evacuation, he recuperated immediately. It was raining heavily and very dark.
An older Jewess left the ramp undetected, fled into a nearby house, got
undressed and sat herself down on a toilet. However, a cleaning woman

---

*obviously the collection point for Jews to be evacuated

Wagen an die Spitze des Zuges gesetzt. Aus Zweckmäßigkeitsgründen
habe ich jedoch die Belegung des Wagens erst bei Tageslicht vornehmen lassen. Die Umrangierung des Begleitwagens war hier nicht
möglich, da der Zug auf dem Hauptgleise stand und sofort abge-
zogen werden musste. Bahnhof Wustermark sollte jedoch Nachricht
erhalten, damit Umrangierung dort erfolgen konnte.
Am 22.12. um 1,15 Uhr wurde Wustermark erreicht. Dieser Bahnhof
sollte jedoch von Stendal keine Nachricht von der Umrangierung erhalten haben. So wurde ich von Bahnhof zu Bahnhof vertröstet, ohne
dass meinem inzwischen als sehr dringend geschilderten Ersuchen
entsprochen wurde. Um 3,30 Uhr hatte der Zug auf der Station
Berlin-Lichterfelde einen Aufenthalt von ½ Stunde. Hier lehnte
man eine Zugleitung eine Umrangierung ohne Angabe näherer Gründe
mit dem Bemerken ab, dass diese erfolgen werde, sofern es sich auf
einem der nächsten Bahnhöfe ermöglichen lässt. Der Zug hatte bereits 105 Minuten Verspätung. Die Fahrt wurde dann über Küstrin,
und Schneidemühl, Firchau fortgesetzt.
Um 16 Uhr habe ich vom Bahnhof Firchau den Bahnhof Konitz ver-
ständigen lassen, dass der Zug dort etwa 1 Stunde Aufenthalt
auf ein Nebengleis nehmen muss, um
a) den leeren Wagen mit Juden zu beladen,
b) die Versorgung der Juden mit Wasser vorzunehmen,
c) die Umrangierung des Begleitwagens zu veranlassen,
d) eine Erfrischung vom Roten Kreuz für die Begleitmannschaft in Empfang zu nehmen.
Der Aufenthalt wurde mir gewährt. Kurz vor Konitz riß der Wagen
wegen seiner Überlastung auseinander. Auch zerriß das Heizungs-
rohr. Der Zug konnte jedoch behelfsmäßig repariert seine. Fahrt
bis Konitz fortsetzen. Um 11,10 Uhr wurde Konitz erreicht. Ich
konnte mein Vorhaben bis auf die Umrangierung des eigenen
Wagens durchführen. Anfänglich wurde mir diese zugesagt, dann
erklärte mir der Stationsvorsteher, dass die Einrangierung des
Wagens in die Mitte des Zuges wegen Fehlens einer Rangierlok.
und der erforderlichen Gleise nicht durchführbar sei, er aber den
Wagen nach vorn rangieren lassen werde. Hiermit war ich unter
den obwaltenden Umständen einverstanden. Nach etwa 5 Minuten
erschien er aber wieder und erklärte mir, dass er den Zug sofort
wieder abfahren lassen müsse und ein Rangieren jetzt, es waren inzwischen 50 Minuten vergangen, nicht mehr möglich sei. Das Verhalten des Stationsvorstehers erschien mir unverständlich, weshalb ich ihn in energischer Weise zur Rede stellte und mich be-
schwerdeführend an die zuständige Aufsichtsstelle wenden wollte.

-4-

had noticed her, so that the Jewess could be apprehended and made to join the transport once more.

By 10:15 A.M. the loading of the Jews was done. After being shunted from track to track, the train left the freightyard of station Duesseldorf-Derendorf in the direction of Wuppertal, already one hour late. After we had left, I noticed that the escort car was placed at the end of the train instead of in the middle. We were thus the twenty-first car, with seven luggage cars behind us. This being placed at the end was to have several negative effects on us.

a) Since the heating system was faulty, the steam pressure did not reach the last few cars. Since it rained incessantly and since it was so cold, the guards' clothing never really dried and I expected them to catch colds.

b) I was in no position to properly watch the train. Even though the floodlights we had brought along were efficient, it was quite a distance the guards had to go before they came to the front of the train. They often had difficulties to reach their own car when the train suddenly started up. On top of this, as soon as the train pulled into a station, the Jews never gave up trying to make overtures to travellers on other trains, either to have them bring water to them or to send out letters. I eventually had to place two guards in a compartment located in one of the cars in front of the train. I had actually complained about all this while still in the freightyard in Duesseldorf, but my complaints went unheeded. We were sent off, as there was no time to rearrange the cars, and I was told that such a rearrangement could be done along the way.

Otherwide, the trip continued as planned and we passed through Wuppertal, Hagen, Schwerte, Hamm. By 6:00 P.M. we reached Hanover-Linden and remained there for almost one hour. I permitted water to be given to some of the Jews, and I asked for the wagons to be.rearranged. First I was told that they would do it, but in the last minute they could not find a locomotive to do the job. They promised, however, to notify the next station so that my request could be granted there. Next, we reached Misterhorst, where, at 9:00 P.M., car 12 was found to have a burned-out axle. The car had to be taken out and the Jews were loaded into the rest of the cars, since there was no substitute

- 4 -

Er erklärte mir darauf, dass diese Stelle für mich nicht zu erreichen sei, er seine Anweisungen habe und den Zug sofort abfahren lassen müsse, weil 2 Gegenzüge zu erwarten seien. Er stellte sogar das Ansinnen an mich, einen Wagen in der Mitte des Zuges von Juden zu räumen, ihn mit meinem Kdo. zu belegen und die Juden im Begleitwagon 2. Klasse unterzubringen. Es erscheint angebracht, diesem Bahnbediensteten von maßgebener Stelle einmal klar zu machen, dass er Angehörige der Deutschen Polizei anders zu behandeln hat als Juden. Ich hatte den Eindruck, als ob es sich bei ihm um einen von denjenigen Vollsgenossen handelt, die noch von den "armen Juden" zu sprechen pflegen und denen der Begriff "Jude" völlig fremd ist. Dieser Bahnbeamte brachte es sogar fertig, den Zug, den ich für 2 Minuten verlassen musste, ... auf der Station des Roten Kreuzes einen Frem.......... aus dem Zug zu entfernen zu lassen, führerlos abfahren zu ......, Nur dem Eingreifen eines meiner Leuten war es zu verdanken, dass der Zug-führer nach dem Anfahren noch einmal hielt und ich den Zug zu noch mit Mühe erreichen konnte. Seine Behauptung, dass Gegen-züge zu erwarten seien, stellte sich als eine leichtsinnige Begründung seines Verhaltens heraus, denn es ist des Kreuzes auf der anschliessenden Fahrt weder ein Gegenzug begegnet, noch sind wir von einem Zug auf einer anderen Haltestation überholt worden.

Die den Transport seit Pirschau begleitenden Bahnbeamten (1. Zug-führer und 1 Schaffner) konnten das Verhalten des Bahnbediensteten in Kreits nicht begreifen. Ihrer Meinung nach als Begleiter über die Umrangierung bei einem Aufenthalt von 1 Stunde ohne einen Zwischenfall ohne weiteres möglich gewesen, wenn nur der gute Wille da gewesen wäre. Sie hatten sich ihm beide zur Hilfe-leistung beim Rangieren zur Verfügung gestellt und den Begleit-wagen bereits abgekuppelt. Um 14,10 Uhr verliess der Zug den Bahnhof Kreits. Die Fahrt führte dann weiter über Dirschau, Marienburg, Elbing nach Königsberg (Pr.). Hier wurde der Zug von 20,12 bis 22 Uhr hin- und herrangiert, ohne dass der Begleit-wagen umrangiert wurde. Auf diesem Bahnhof erreichte mich die Meldung, dass ein Wagen 17 ein Kind am Sterben sei. Nach näherer Vorstellung durch die begleitende jüdische Ärztin hatte es ein 14-jähriges Mädchen mit Darmausscheidungen gelegentlich der Periode zu tun. Um 22,10 Uhr (21.12.) wurde die Fahrt fortgesetzt, ... vor Insterburg Ulikner Zug übernahm angekuppelt. Beide Teile des Zuges wurden zur Station Insterburg geschleppt werden, wo der betreffende Wagen 15 ausgewechselt und die Juden in den neu-

-5-

car available. The sleeping Jews did not appreciate this procedure at all. As it was already dark and the rain kept coming down, matters proved to be rather difficult at first, but by applying proper pressure, we got through the whole thing quickly. During the transfer, the floodlights came in handy.

By 11:00 P.M., we reached Stendal where they gave us an empty car; it was put at the head of the train, but I was going to wait for daylight before attempting yet another transfer. As for my own car, it could not be moved since the train was standing on one of the main tracks and had to leave immediately. They promised to inform station Wustermark about my plight. We arrived there on December 12, at 1:15 A.M., but they said that they had not received any message from Stendal. In this way, from station to station, all I got was promises, despite my urgent requests. At 3:30 A.M., the train reached Berlin-Lichterfelde, where it stayed for half an hour. They refused to move my car without giving me any reasons. All they said was that I would have to wait for another station, where such a move could be effected. By then, our train was almost 3 hours behind schedule.

The next cities we passed were Kuestrin, Schneidemuehle and Pirchau. From the last one I got in touch with Konitz, the next stop, and asked if I could get an hour's time on an auxiliary track so that I would be able to:

a) load the empty car in front with Jews,
b) arrange for the Jews to get water,
c) have my own car moved, and
d) get some refreshments for the guards from the Red Cross.

I was granted this time, but shortly before we reached Konitz, one of the cars broke down because it was overloaded and the heating system broke down as well. All was repaired after a fashion and the train could continue on to Konitz, which it reached by 11:10 A.M. I could do all I had planned on, except move my own car. At first, they had promised to do it, but then the stationmaster explained to me that he had neither a locomotive nor enough tracks to effect such a transfer and put my car into the middle of the train. He would, however, bring it to the front of

- 5 -

bereitgestellten Wagen umgeladen wurden. Um 1,50 Uhr ging es
weiter nach Tilsit. Auf dieser Station nahe der ostpr.litauischen
Grenze wurde auf meine erneute Bitte in Insterburg hin der Wagen
des Begleitkdos. nach vorn rangiert und erhielt endlich Heizung.
Die Wärme wurde von der Begleitmannschaft sehr wohltuend empfunden,
da die Uniformen der Posten infolge des auf der ganzen Fahrt fast
ununterbrochen anhaltenden Regens völlig durchnässt und nunmehr
getrocknet werden konnten. Um 5,15 Uhr wurde die Grenzstation
Keigenenger und nach 15 Minuten die litauische Station Tauroggen
erreicht. Von hier aus sollte die Fahrt bis Riga normal nur noch
24 Stunden betragen. Infolge des eingleisigen Bahngeländes und
der Schwierigkeit des Zuges in der Abfertigung gab es auf den
Teilstücken oft lange Verzögerungen in der Weiterfahrt. Auf dem
Bahnhof Schaulen (1,12 Uhr) wurde die Begleitmannschaft von
Schwestern des Roten Kreuzes ausreichend und gut verpflegt. Es
wurde Suppe mit Rindfleisch verabfolgt. In Schaulen wurde
in allen Judenwagen durch litauisches Eisenbahnpersonal die
Notbremsur abgestellt. Auf dem nächsten Bahnhof hatte ich Gelegenheit, die Juden letztmalig aus einem in der Nähe liegenden
Brunnen Wasser fassen zu lassen. Das Wasser auf litauischen und
lettischen Bahnhöfen ist durchweg ungekocht genießbar, nur
schwierig erreichbar, da Brunnen nicht immer in der Nähe des Bahn-
körpers liegen und Zapfstellen nach deutschem Muster nicht vorhanden sind.

Um 19,50 Uhr wurde Mitau (Lettland) erreicht. Hier machte sich
schon eine erheblich kühlere Temperatur bemerkbar. Es setzte
Schneetreiben mit anschließendem Frost ein. Die Ankunft in Riga
erfolgte um 21,50 Uhr, wo der Zug auf dem Bahnhof 1 ½ Stunden
festgehalten wurde. Hier stellte ich fest, dass die Juden nicht
für das Rigaer Ghetto bestimmt waren, sondern in Ghetto Skirotawa,
8 km nordostwärts von Riga, untergebracht werden sollten.

Am 13.12., um 23,35 Uhr, erreichte der Zug nach vielen Hin- und
Herrangieren die Militärrampe auf dem Bahnhof Skirotawa. Der Zug
blieb ungeheizt stehen. Die Außentemperatur betrug bereits
12° unter Null. Da ein Übernahmekdo. der Stapo nicht zur Stelle
war, wurde die Bewachung des Zuges vorläufig von meinen Männern
weiter durchgeführt. Die Übergabe des Zuges erfolgte alsdann um
1,45 Uhr, gleichzeitig wurde die Bewachung von 6 lettischen Polizei-
männern übernommen. Da es bereits nach Mitternacht war, Dunkelheit
herrschte und die Verladerampe stark vereist war, sollte die
Ausladung und die Überführung der Juden in das noch 2 km entfernt

the train, a suggestion to which I agreed. Five minutes later, he came back and said that it would no longer be possible to move the car since the train had to leave immediately. We had been there about 50 minutes. I could not understand his behavior and I firmly remonstrated with him, threatening that I would complain to the district authorities. He replied that I could not reach his superiors, that he had his orders and that our train had better leave as he expected two trains from the opposite direction. He even suggested that I empty my second class car and transfer my guards and myself into the middle car, from which I should expel the Jews and put them into my car. Their car of course was only third class. I believe that this stationmaster should be made to realize through proper channels, that he is to treat members of the German police differently from Jews. I had the impression that he was one of those citizens who still talk about "poor Jews" and to whom the true concept of "Jew" is unknown. To add insult to injury, I left the train for two minutes in order to have the Red Cross personnel remove a foreign body from my eye, and the stationmaster went so far as to let the train leave without me. Thanks to one of my guards who noticed my absence and made the driver stop the train, I could just reach it. As for the stationmaster's allegation about expected trains from the opposite side, our train did not encounter another one on our subsequent trip, nor did another train overtake us.

The two railroad officials who had accompanied our train from the beginning, were rather puzzled by the Konitz stationmaster's behavior. Being experts, both agreed that a transfer of cars during the hour of our stay in Konitz would no doubt have been possible, if there had been some good will present. In fact, these two had already separated the last car from the rest of the train. At any rate, we left Konitz at 12:10, passed Marienburg and Elbing and arrived at 8:00 P.M. in Koenigsberg, Prussia. There, the train was shunted about for around two hours; nothing, however, was done about my car. I was told that in car 17 a child lay dying. After checking with the transport's Jewish woman doctor, I found that the girl suffered from heart spasms brought on by her period. We continued on our way at 10:10. Shortly before Insterburg, the coupling broke once more and both parts of the train had to be towed there. Car 15 was taken out, and the Jews were put into a newly prepared one.

liegende Sammelghetto erst am Sonntag früh beim Hellwerden erfolgen.
Mein Begleitkdo. wurde durch 2 von Kdo. d.Sch. bereitgestellte
Pol.-Streifenwagen nach Riga gebracht und bezog dort gegen 3 Uhr
Nachtquartier. Ich selbst erhielt Unterkunft in Gästehaus des
Höh.H- und Pol.-Führers, Petersburger Hof, an Schloßplatz 4.

2.) Aufenthalt in Riga.

Mit Rücksicht auf die während des Transportes durchnäßte und
verschmutzte Bekleidung der Waffen und des Geräts setzte ich für
den 14. 12. von 13 - 16 Uhr Waffenreinigen und Instandsetzen der
Bekleidung und Ausrüstung an. Vorher gab ich den Männern Gelegenheit, in einem in der Nähe ihrer Unterkunft gelegenen Lokal
warme" Mittagessen einzunehmen. Lebensmittelmarken wurden mir
von Bdo. in Riga zur Verfügung gestellt. Den Rückmarsch des
Begleitkdos. mußte ich auf den 15. 12. um 15,01 Uhr festsetzen.
Da täglich nur dieser eine Zug von Riga nach Tilsit für Wehr-
machtsangehörige verkehrt und ich die mitgeführten RM 50 000
Judengelder dem Geldverwalter der Stapo am 15.12. früh noch zu
übergeben hatte.

Die Stadt Riga ist durch den Krieg so gut wie unversehrt ge-
blieben. Mit Ausnahme der gesprengten Dünabrücken und einiger
in der Nähe gelegenen zerschossenen Häuser der Altstadt habe ich
weitere Beschädigungen nicht bemerkt. Riga umfasst etwa 360 000
Einwohner, darunter befanden sich etwa 35 000 Juden. Die Juden
waren in der Geschäftswelt wie überall führend. Ihre Geschäfte sind
jedoch sogleich nach dem Einmarsch der deutschen Truppen geschlossen
und beschlagnahmt worden. Die Juden selbst wurden in einem durch
Stacheldraht abgeschlossenen Ghetto an der Düna untergebracht. Z.Zt.
sollen sich in diesem Ghetto nur 2 500 männliche Juden, die als
Arbeitskräfte verwendet werden, befinden. Die übrigen Juden sind
einer anderen zweckentsprechenden Verwendung zugeführt bezw. von
den Letten erschossen worden.

Riga ist städtebaulich eine sehr schöne Stadt, die sich mit
jeder Stadt des Reiches messen kann. Das Verkehrs- und Wirtschafts-
leben ist bereits geordnet. Es sind seit einiger Zeit Kleider-
und Lebensmittelkarten eingeführt worden. Die Lebensmittel pp.
sind dort sehr billig. So kostete ein ausreichendes Mittagessen
50 - 75 Pfennige. Das lettische Volk ist, soweit ich beobachten
konnte, deutschfreundlich und spricht auch zum grossen Teil
deutsch. Vielfach war aber aus dem Verhalten von Einzelpersön-
lichkeiten erkennbar, dass sie dem zaristischen Rußland noch
immer in Treue ergeben sind. Von den Bolschewisten will jedoch
kein Lette etwas wissen, da es selten eine Familie gibt, die

-7-

December 13. At 1:50 A.M. we went on to Tilsit. At that station, near the Eastprussian/Lithuanian border, my car was finally moved to the front and thus could obtain heat. This was greatly appreciated by the guards whose uniforms were soaked. Finally, they could think of drying them. By 5:15 A.M. we reaced the border and 15 minutes later stopped at the Lithuanian town of Tauroggen. Normally, the trip from there to Riga should last only 14 hours, but since there were sometimes only single tracks, travelling became time-consuming. At 1:12 P.M. we reach Schaulen. The Red Cross nurses gave us a delicious and plentiful dinner, consisting of barley soup with beef. Meanwhile, the Lithuanian railroad personnel turned off all the lights in the waggons occupied by Jews. At the next station, I had the opportunity to let the Jews get water from a well nearby. The water in Lituania and Latvia can be ingested without boiling it first, but at the stations it is hard to get to, since the wells are not always close by and there are no fountains as there are in Germany.

By 7:30 P.M. we reached Mitau, Latvia. It got to be extremely cold and we had snow and frost. At 10:10 we reached Riga and the train was kept there for over an hour. I found out that the Jews were not meant to go to the ghetto in Riga, but to one in Skirotava, [sic] 8 km north-west of the city. By 11:35 P.M., after being moved about for a while, the train reached the military ramp of station Skirotava and was left to stand there without heat while the outside temperature had already fallen to 12 degrees Celsius below zero. As there was no one from the State Police there to take over, my men continued to watch the train. At 2:00 A.M. we finally handed the train over and the watch was taken over by 6 Latvian policemen. Since it was long past midnight and very dark, and also since the ramp was a sheet of ice, the unloading of the Jews was postponed until Sunday morning, when it would be light and when they could be brought into their ghetto 2 km away. My men were taken to Riga by car and reached their quarters by 3:00 A.M. I was given lodgings at the guest-house of the Higher SS and Police Command, Petersburger Hof, Schlossplatz 4.

2) Stay in Riga

As my men's uniforms and weapons had suffered from moisture and dirt on the way, I ordered them to use the afternoon of the 14th for a

- 7 -

während der Besetzung durch die Sowjets ohne Blutopfer davonge-
kommen ist. Ihr Hass gilt insbesondere den Juden. Sie haben sich
daher von Zeitpunkt der Befreiung bis jetzt auch sehr ausgiebig
an der Ausrottung dieser Parasiten beteiligt. Es erscheint ihnen
aber, was ich insbesondere beim lettischen Eisenbahnpersonal
feststellen konnte, unverständlich, weshalb Deutschland die
Juden nach Lettland bringt und sie nicht im eigenen Lande aus-
rottete.

Die Strassen in Riga dürfen von der Bevölkerung während der Nacht
ohne Passierschein nicht betreten werden. Zu Schießereien ist es
in der letzten Zeit nicht mehr gekommen. Auf dem flachen Lande
soll dieses jedoch noch immer der Fall sein. Zum Teil handelt
es sich bei den Runruhestiftern um alte Kommunisten, zum Teil aber
auch um von den Sowjets durch Fallschirm abgesetzte Saboteure in
Zivil. Zur Bekämpfung dieses Gesindels sind Pol.Batl. in aus-
reichendem Umfange eingesetzt. In Riga selbst befinden sich sehr
viele Stäbe der Nachschubeinheiten der Wehrmacht und auch solche
der Polizei.

Pol.-Truppenverbände sind in Riga nicht stationiert.

3.) Rückmarsch des Begleitkommandos.

Die Innarschsetzung des Begleitkdos. nach Düsseldorf erfolgte am
15.12. mit dem um 15,01 Uhr nach Tilsit verkehrenden Zug. Der Zug
war durch Weihnachtsurlauber stark besetzt und traf erst am
16.12. um 8 Uhr in Tilsit ein. Immerhin brauchte er für die
360 km lange Fahrtstrecke 17 Stunden. Nach einem Aufenthalt von
3 Stunden verlief die Fahrt ab Tilsit mit den fahrplanmäßigen
Zügen über Insterburg, Königsberg, Marienburg, Dirschau reibungs-
los. Am 17.12. um 0,06 Uhr wurde Berlin erreicht. Bereits um 0,30 Uhr
konnte ab Berlin ein Urlaubszug benutzt werden, der über Hannover,
Hamm und Dortmund geleitet wurde und um 13 Uhr Düsseldorf erreichte. Die gesamte Rückfahrzeit ab Riga betrug 46 Stunden,
während für die Hinfahrt mit dem Sonderzug 61 Stunden benötigt
wurden.

4.) Erfahrungen.
   a) Die mitgegebene Verpflegung war gut und ausreichend.
   b) Die Mitnahme von 2 Decken, Kochgeschirren, Petroleumkocher,
      warmer Kleidung, Postenpelzen und Filzstiefeln kam den Männern
      sehr zu statten und ist auch für künftige Transporte wünschens-
      wort.
   c) Die Bewaffnung mit Pistolen und Karabinern war ausreichend,
      da in Litauen und Lettland Überfälle durch Partisanen auch

-8-

thorough cleaning. Before doing so, I let them have a warm meal in a restaurant near their quarters. Rationcards were supplied by the Riga authorities. I arranged our departure for the 15th at 3:00 P.M., since that train was the only one to leave Riga for Tilsit open to soldiers. I also needed the morning of the 15th to give the 50,000 Reichsmark Jewmoney to the treasurer of the state police.

The city of Riga has not been ravaged by war and except for the dynamited bridges and a few destroyed houses in the old city, I did not notice any damages. Riga has approximately 360,000 inhabitants. Of these, there had been 35,000 Jews. As all over, the Jews were the leading businessmen. Their stores, however, were confiscated and closed immediately after the arrival of German troops. The Jews were put into a ghetto, secured by barbed wire, near the Duena. At this time, this ghetto holds only about 2,500 Jewish males who are used for labor. The others have been used for another purpose, i.e., they were shot by the Latvians.

Architecturally, Riga is a beautiful city and can compare with any city in the Reich. Transportation and economic circumstances are already well ordered and for some time now, rationing for clothing and food has been introduced. Food is very cheap. A good dinner costs only 50-75 Pfennige. As far as I could see, the Latvians like the Germans and most of them speak German. Some of them, however, made it clear by their attitude that they are still loyal to tsarist Russia. None of them want to be reminded of the Bolsheviks. Almost every family here had to pay a bloody price during the Soviet occupation. The Latvians hate the Jews with a vengeance and for this reason, ever since their liberation, have taken a great part in the extermination of these parasites. As I could ascertain by talking to the Latvian railroad personnel, they cannot understand why the Germans bring Jews to Latvia instead of exterminating them in their own country.

People must have passes in order to be on the streets in Riga after dark. Lately, though, there were no more shootings in the city itself. In rural districts, however, this is still the case, mainly caused by troublemakers, who may either be Latvian hard-line communists, or even civilian Soviets, who were dropped by parachute. To fight this rabble, there are

- 8 -

zu befürchten sind. Dagegen ist die Bewaffnung des Begleitkdos.
mit M.P.s, l.MG,s oder Handgranaten erforderlich, wenn Transporte
nach Städten geleitet werden, die in ehemals russischen Gebiet
liegen.

d) Die beiden Handscheinwerfer haben sich gut bewährt. Ihre Mitnahme halte ich auch bei künftigen Transporten für unbedingt
erforderlich. Ihre Anwendung habe ich vom Zuge aus vornehmen lassen,
da sie für die Posten selbst sehr hinderlich waren und einen etwaigen
Gebrauch der Schußwaffe in Frage stellten.

5) Ebenso ist die Ausrüstung der Männer mit Taschenlampen, Ersatz-
batterien sowie die Mitnahme von Kerzen als Notbeleuchtung nach wie
vor erforderlich.

e) Die Unterstützung durch das Rote Kreuz muss ich lobend erwähnen.
Inbezug auf die Verabreichung von Erfrischungen ist dem Kdo. von
den in Anspruch genommenen Stationen jede nur erdenkliche Unterstützung zuteil geworden.

f) Zur Verabfolgung von Trinkwasser für die Juden ist es unbedingt
erforderlich, dass die Gestapo mit der Reichsbahn für je einen Tag
des Transportes 1 Stunde Aufenthalt auf einem geeigneten Bahnhof
des Reichsgebiets vereinbart. Es hat sich herausgestellt, dass die
Reichsbahn wegen des festgelegten Fahrplanes nur mit Widerwillen
auf entsprechende Wünsche des Transportführers eingeht. Die Juden
sind gewöhnlich vor Abgang des Transportes 14 Stunden und länger
unterwegs und haben die mitgenommenen Getränke vor der Abfahrt bereits aufgebraucht. Bei einer Nichtversorgung mit Wasser während
des Transportes versuchen sie dann, trotz Verbot, bei jeder sich
bietenden Gelegenheit aus dem Zuge zu gelangen, um sich Wasser zu
holen oder holen zu lassen.

g) Es ist ferner dringend erforderlich, dass die Reichsbahn die Züge
rechtzeitig, mindestens 3 - 4 Stunden vor der festgesetzten Abfahrts-
zeit bereitstellt, damit die Einladung der Juden und ihres Gepäcks
geordnet erfolgen kann.

Vor allem ist von der Gestapo mit der Reichsbahn zu verein-
baren, dass der gestellte Wagen für das Begleitkdo. (2.Kl.) gleich
bei der Zusammenstellung in die Mitte des Zuges einrangiert wird.
Diese Einrangierung ist aus Gründen der sicheren Überwachung
des Transportes dringend notwendig. In anderen Falle ergeben sich
die in Ziff. 1 geschilderten Schwierigkeiten. Bei starker Kälte
ist darauf zu achten, dass die Beheizungsanlagen des Zuges in
Ordnung sind.

-9-

police batallions galore. The same is true of Riga, which as an enormous amount of military and police personnel.

3) Return of the Guards

We started our trip back to Duesseldorf by taking the 3:00 P.M. train of Dec. 15 from Riga to Tilsit. It was very crowded by soldiers going on Christmas vacation, and we arrived in Tilsit on the 16th, at 8 in the morning (17 hours for a distance of 360 km). We left three hours later, and the rest of the trip went according to schedule over Insterburg, Koenigsberg, Marienburg and Dirschau. In Berlin we got into a special vacation train, passed through Hanover, Hamm and Dortmund, reaching Duesseldorf at 1:00 P.M. The total return trip took 46 hours. The trip to Riga, in the special train, took 61 hours.

4) Comments:

a) The food we had taken along was good and plentiful.

b) The men were glad to have 2 blankets each, furs and felt boots. All this came in very handy and should be taken along on future transports.

c) Pistols and rifles were sufficient for Lithuania and Latvia, since partisan attacks are only a possibility. For transports to cities on former Russian territory, additional weapons such as machine pistols and howitzers as well as handgranades should be supplied.

d) The two floodlights we had taken along were very much appreciated. I believe that they should be required for future transports. The way I used them was from the train itself, rather than by the guards, who would have been prevented from using their weapons if their hands had not been free.

e) Now and in the future, the guards should be supplied with flash-lights, batteries, and even candles for emergency situations.

f) I would like to make grateful mention of the help I received from the Red Cross and especially for the kindness with which they offered us refreshments along the way.

OLICE D'ISRAEL   משטרת ישראל
IARTIER GENERAL   4ème BUREAU   המטה הארצי לשכה 06   138

~ 9 ~

5.) Die gestellten Männer des Begleitkommandos haben zu nennenswerten
Klagen keinen Anlass gegeben. Abgesehen davon, dass ich einzelne
von ihnen zu schärferen Vorgehen gegen Juden, die meine er-
lassenen Verbote zu übertreten glaubten, anhalten musste, haben
sich alle sehr gut geführt und ihren Dienst einwandfrei versehen.
Krankmeldungen oder Zwischenfälle sind nicht vorgekommen.

                              gez.: Salitter
                         Hauptmann der Schutzpolizei.

g) To supply the Jews with drinking water, it is by all means necessary that the Gestapo and railroad agree on at least one hour's time per day at a most likely stop. I found out that railroad officials, because of rigid schedules, are not willing to listen to the demands of transport leaders. In our case, the Jews most likely had been moved around for at least 14 hours prior to deportation and had therefore used up all the liquids they had taken along. If we do not supply them with water during the trip, they try to get out of the train at every opportunity, even when they are forbidden to do so. They try to get water either by themselves or by having someone get it for them.

h) Furthermore, it is very important to have the railroad prepare the trains at least 3 or 4 hours before the listed departure, so that the loading of the Jews and their luggage can proceed in an orderly manner. The Gestapo should also see to it that the second class car for the guards be placed in the middle of the train. For reasons of security, this is of utmost importance. If this is not arranged, then the above mentioned difficulties may occur. Also, if it is very cold, all efforts should be made for the heating system of the train to function properly.

5) I have no special complaints about the accompanying guards, except perhaps for the fact that I had to remind some of them to treat the Jews in a sharper manner whenever they disobeyed my orders.

Other than that, the guards behaved well and did their duty in the proper manner. There were no sicknesses to report, nor were they any further unexpected events.

Signed
SALITTER
Captain of Police

Works to Be Consulted for Further Reference

PRIMARY SOURCES

I. Nazi Germany

Dokumente der deutschen Politik und Geschichte. Berlin, 1953

Dokumente ueber die Behandlung der Juden durch das dritte Reich. Duesseldorf: Verlag Allgemeine Wochenzeitung der Juden in Deutschland, 1958.

Hofer, Walter. *Der Nationalsozialismus: Dokumente 1933 bis 1945.* Frankfurt am Main, 1957.

Rueckerl, Adalbert. *NS Prozesse.* Karlsruhe: Verlag C.F. Mueller, 1971.

SS im Einsatz: Eine Dokumentation ueber die Verbrechen der SS. Berlin: Deutscher Militaerverlag, 1964.

The Goebbels Diaries. London: H. Hamilton, Ltd., 1948.

II. Miscellaneous Topics: Monographs and Documents

Braham, Randolph L., ed. *The Destruction of Hungarian Jewry: A Documentary Account.* New York: Pro Arte Publishers for the World Federation of Hungarian Jews, 1963.

Der Prozess gegen die Hauptkriegsverbrecher vor dem Internationalen Militaergerichtshof. International Military Tribunal; volumes of special interest to Riga are numbers III, VI, VII, XXIX, XXX, XXXIX. Nuernberg, 1948.

Dokumenty i Materialy. 3 vols. Warsaw, Lodz, and Krakow: The Central Jewish Historical Commission, 1946.

Piotrowski, Stanislaw. *The Diary of Hans Frank.* Warsaw: Polskie Wydenie Narodowe, 1963.

The Black Book: The Nazi Crimes against the Jewish People. New York: Duel, Sloan, and Pearce, Inc., 1946.

Verbrecherische Ziele - Verbrecherische Mittel: Dokumente der Okkupationspolitik des faschistischen Deutschlands auf dem Territorium der U.S.S.R. 1941 - 1944. Moscow: Verlag fuer fremdsprachige Literatur, 1963.

III. The Ghettos

Adler, H.G. *Die Verheimlichte Wahrheit: Theresienstaedter Dokumente.* Tuebingen: J.C.B. Mohr (Paul Siebeck), 1958.

Adler, H.G. *Theresienstadt 1941 - 1945: Das Antlitz einer Zwangsgemeinschaft.* Tuebingen: J.C.B. Mohr (Paul Siebeck), 1955.

Auerbach, Rahel. *Der yidisher oyfstand in varshe 1943* [The Jewish Uprising in Warsaw]. Warsaw: Zentral Komitet fun Poylishe Yidn, 1948.

Boehm, Eric, ed. *We Survived.* 20th Century Series. Santa Barbara, California: Clio Press, 1966.

Bozykowski, Tovye. *Tsvishn falendike vent* [Between Falling Walls]. Warsaw: Hechalutz, 1949.

Dworzecki, Mark. *Zikhroynes fun vilner geto* [Stories from the Vilna Ghetto]. Paris: Yidisher Folksverband, 1948.

Gar, Joseph. *Umkum fun der yidisher kovne* [Destruction of Jewish Kovno]. Munich: Farband fun Litvishe Yidn, 1948.

Goldstein, Bernard. *The Stars Bear Witness.* Translated from the Yiddish. New York: Viking, 1949. Paper edition as *Five Years in the Warsaw Ghetto.* New York: Dolphin Books, 1961.

Hirschhorn, Traudl. "Fahrt ins Grauen." *Der Neue Weg,* vol. I (March 1946), 3-10.

Kaplan, Chaim Aron. *Scroll of Agony.* Edited and translated by A.I. Katsh. New York: Macmillan, 1965.

Kaufmann, Max. *Die Vernichtung der Juden Lettlands.* Munich: Deutscher Verlag, 1947.

Lederer, Zdenek. *Ghetto Theresienstadt.* London: Edward Goldstone & Son, Ltd., 1953.

Neustadt, Melekh. *Khurben un oyfshtand fun die yidn in varshe* [Tragedy and resistence of Jews in Warsaw]. 2 vols. Tel Aviv: Histadrut, 1948.

Pawlowicz, Sala with Kevin Klose. *I Will Survive.* New York: W.W. Norton & Company, Inc., 1962.

Sloan, Jacob, ed. and trans. *Notes from the Warsaw Ghetto: The Journal of Emmanuel Ringelblum.* New York: McGraw-Hill, 1958.

Trunk, Isaiah. *Lodzer geto.* New York: Yivo, 1962.

Turkow, Jonas. *Azoy is es geven: Khurbn varshe* [This is how it was]. 2 vols. Buenos Aires: Zentral Farband fun Poylishe Yidn, 1948-1950.

Wolff, Jeanette. *Sadismus oder Wahnsinn.* Dresden: Sachsenverlag Druckerei, 1946.

IV. Concentration Camps

Bericht des Internationalen Lagerkomitees Buchenwald. Weimar: Thueringer Volksverlag, 1945.

Borowski, Tadeusz. *This Way for the Gas, Ladies and Gentlemen, and other stories.* Translated from the Polish. London: Jonathan Cape, 1967.

Commandant of Auschwitz: The Autobiolography of Rudolf Hess. Translated from the German. New York: Popular Library, 1961.

Donat, Alexander. *The Holocaust Kingdom: A Memoir.* New York: Holt, Rinehart and Winston, 1963.

Erinnerungen Auschwitzer Haeftlinge. Translated from the Polish. Krakow: Verlag Panstowowe Muzeum W Oswiecimiu, 1960.

Kaczkowski, Adam. *Auschwitz-Birkenau.* Krakow: Drukarnia Narodowa, 1947.

Kogon, Eugen. *Der SS Staat: Das System der deutschen Konzentrationslager.* Stockholm: Bermann-Fischer Verlag, 1947. English Paperback entitled *The Theory and Practice of Hell.* Berkley Publishing Co., 1950.

Kolb, Eberhard. *Bergen-Belsen.* Hanover: Verlag fuer Literatur und Zeitgeschehen, 1962.

Lengyel, Olga. *Five Chimneys: The Story of Auschwitz, I Survived Hitler's Ovens.* New York: Avon, 1948.

Levi, Primo. *If this is a Man.* Translated from the Italian. New York: Orion Press, 1959. Paperback edition entitled *Survival in Auschwitz: The Nazi Assault on Humanity* New York: Colliers, 1961.

March, Tony, ed. *Darkness Over Europe: First Person Accounts of Life in Europe during the War Years 1939 - 1945.* Chicago: Rand McNally & Co., 1969.

Nyiszli, Dr. Milos. *Auschwitz: A Doctor's Eyewitness Account.* Translated from the Hungarian. Greenwich, Conn.: Fawcett Crest Books, 1960.

Poller, Walter. *Arztschreiber in Buchenwald.* Hamburg: Phoenix Verlag Christen & Co., 1947.

Reder, Rudolf, *Belzec.* Krakow: Centralna Zydowska Komisja Historyczna przy C.K. Zydow Polskich, 1946.

Shtrigler, M. *In die fabrikn fun toyt.* Buenos Aires: Zentral Farband fun Poylishe Yidn, 1948.

Shtrigler M. *Majdanek.* Buenos Aires: Zentral Farband fun Poylishe Yidn, 1947.

Steiner, Jean-Francois. *Treblinka.* Translated from the French. New York: Simon and Schuster, 1967.

Vrba, Rudolf and Alan Bestic. *I Cannot Forgive.* New York: Grove Press, Inc., 1964.

Wells, Leon Weliczker. *The Janowska Road.* New York: McMillan Co., 1963.

Wiesel, Elie. *Night.* Translated from the French. New York: Avon, 1969.

SECONDARY SOURCES

I. Bibliographies

Robinson, Jacob and Friedman, Philip, eds. *Guide to Jewish History under Nazi Impact.* Yad Vashem and Yivo Joint Documentary Project, Bibliographical Series, no. 1. New York: 1960.

Robinson, Jacob and Bauer, Yehuda, eds. *Guide to Unpublished Materials of the Holocaust Period.* Jerusalem: 1970.

Wolff, Ilse R., ed. *Books on Persecution, Terror and Resistance in Nazi Germany.* The Wiener Library Catalogue Series, no. 1. 2d rev. ed. London: 1960.

Wolff, Ilse R., ed. *German Jewry, Its History, Life and Culture.* The Wiener Library Catalogue Series, no. 3. London: 1958.

II. Comprehensive Works and Interpretations

Arendt, Hannah. *Eichmann in Jerusalem: A Report on the Banality of Evil.* Rev. ed. New York: Viking, 1964.

Bettelheim, Bruno. *The Informed Heart: Anatomy in a Mass Age.* Glencoe, Ill.: The Free Press, 1960.

Das Wanness Protokoll zur Endloesung der Judenfrage und einige Fragen an die, die es angeht. Duesseldorf, 1952.

Dawidowicz, Lucy S. "Toward a History of the Holocaust." *Commentary,* XLVII, 4 (April 1969), 51-56.

Die Kontroverse: Hannah Arendt, Eichmann, und die Juden. Munich: Nymphenburger Verlagshandlung, 1964.

Dubnow, S.M. *History of the Jews in Russia and Poland.* Translated from the Russian by I. Friedlaender. Philadelphia: The Jewish Publication Society of America, 1916.

Hilberg, Raul. *The Destruction of the European Jews.* With a new postscript by the author. Chicago: Quadrangle Paperback, 1967.

Levin, Nora. *The Holocaust.* New York: Thomas Y. Crowell Company, 1968.

Nellessen, Bernd. *Der Prozess von Jerusalem.* Dusseldorf and Vienna: Econ Verlag, 1964.

Page, Stanley W. *The Formation of the Baltic States: A Study of the effects of great power politics upon the emergence of Lithuania, Latvia, and Estonia.* Cambridge, Mass.: Harvard University Press, 1959.

Poliakow, Leon. *Harvest of Hate: The Nazi Program for the Destruction of the Jews of Europe.* Translated from the French. Syracuse, New York: Syracuse University Press, 1954.

Reitlinger, Gerald. *The Final Solution: The Attempt to Exterminate the Jews of Europe 1939 - 1945.* South Brunswick, New Jersey: Thomas Yoseloff, 1961.

Robinson, Jacob. *And the Crooked Shall be made Straight: The Eichmann Trail, the Jewish Catastrophe, and Hannah Arendt's Narrative.* New York: Macmillan, 1965.

III. Nazi Germany

Arendt, Hannah. *The Origins of Totalitariansim.* 2d rev. ed. Cleveland and New York: The World Publishing Co., Meridian Books, 1958.

Bracher, Karl Dietrich. *The German Dictatorship: Origin, Structure, and Effects of National Socialism.* Translated from the German. New York: Praeger, 1970.

Bracher, Karl Dietrich, Wolfgang Sauer, and Gerhard Schulz. *Die natiolsozialistische Machtergreifung: Studien zur Errichtung des totalitaeren Herrschaftssystems in Deutschland, 1933-34.* Cologne and Opladen: Westdeutscher Verlag, 1962.

Bullock, Alan. *Hitler: A Study in Tyranny.* London: Odhams Press, 1952.

Crankshaw, Edward. *Gestapo.* New York: Viking Press, 1956.

Das Ausnahmerecht fuer die Juden in den Europaeischen Laendern 1933-1945. Bearbeitet von Bruno Blau. New York, 1952.

Dallin, Alexander. *German Rule in Russia, 1941 - 1945: A Study of Occupation Policies.* New York: St. Martin's Press, 1957.

Friedman, Philip. "Research and Literature on the Recent Jewish Tragedy." *Jewish Social Studies,* XII, 1 (January 1950), 17-26.

Friedrich, Carl J., ed. *Totalitarianism*. New York: Grosset and Dunlap, University Library, 1964.

Harris, Whitney R. *Tyranny on Trial*. Dallas, Texas: Southern Methodist University Press, 1954.

Heiden Konrad. *Der Fuehrer: Hitler's Rise to Power*. Translated from the German by Ralph Mannheim. Boston: Houghton Mifflin, 1944.

Kempner, Robert M.W. *Das Dritte Reich im Kreuzverhoer*. Munich: Bechtle Verlag, 1969.

Kinser, Bill and Neil Kleinman. *The Dream That Was No More A Dream: A Search for Aesthetic Reality in Germany, 1890 - 1945*. New York: Harper and Row, Colophon Books, 1969.

Klemperer, Victor. *Notizbuch eines Philologen*. Berlin: Aufbau Verlag, 1946.

Langbein, Hermann. *Im Namen des Deutschen Volkes*. Vienna: Europa Verlag, 1963.

Langbein, Hermann. *Wir Haben Es Getan*. Vienna: Europa Verlag, 1964.

Mosse, George L. *The Crisis of German Ideology: Intellectual Origins of the Third Reich*. New York: Grosset and Dunlap, Universal Library, 1964.

Neumann, Franz. *Behemoth: The Structure and Practice of National Socialism* New York: Harper and Row Torchbooks, 1965.

Pinson, Koppel S. *Modern Germany: Its History and Civilization*. New York: Macmillan, 1954.

Poliakov, Leon and Joseph Wulf. *Das Dritte Reich und die Juden: Dokumente und Aufsaetze*. Berlin: Arani, 1955.

Reitlinger, Gerald. *The SS: Alibi of a Nation. 1922-1945.* New York: Viking, Compass Books, 1957.

Snyder, Louis L. *Hitler and Nazism.* New York and Canada: Franklin Watts, Inc., A Bantam Book, 1961.

Stern, Fritz. *The Politics of Cultural Despair: A Study in the Rise of the Germanic Ideology.* Garden City, New York: Doubleday, Anchor Books, 1965.

Taylor, Telford. *Sword and Swastika: Generals and Nazis in the Third Reich.* New York: Simon and Schuster, 1952.

Viereck, Peter. *Metapolitics: The Roots of the Nazi Mind.* New York: Capricorn Books, 1961.

Weinreich, Max. *Hitler's Professors.* New York: Yivo, 1946.

Wheeler-Bennett, John W. *The Nemesis of Power: The German Army in Politics, 1918 - 1945.* New York: Viking, Compass Books, 1967.

World Jewish Congress. *Hitler's Ten Year War on the Jews.* New York: International Press, 1943.

IV. Anti-Semitism

Adorno, T.W. and others. *The Authoritarian Personality.* New York: Harper, 1950.

Cohn, Norman. *Warrant for Genocide: The Myth of the Jewish World Conspiracy and the Protocol of the Elders of Zion.* New York: Harper and Row Torchbooks, 1969.

Hay, Malcolm. *The Foot of Pride: The Pressure of Christendom on the People of Israel for 1900 Years.* Boston: Beacon, 1950.

Heer, Friedrich. *God's First Love.* New York: Weybright & Talley, 1970.

Massing, Paul R. *Rehearsal for Destruction: A Study of Political Anti-Semitism in Imperial Germany.* New York: Harper, 1949.

Parkes, James. *Antisemitism.* Chicago: Quadrangle, 1969.

Pinson, Koppel, ed. *Essays on Anti-Semitism.* 2d rev. ed. New York: Conference on Jewish Relations, 1946.

Poliakov, Leon. *A History of Anti-Semitism.* Translated from the French. New York: Vanguard, 1964.

Pulzer, Peter G.J. *The Rise of Political Anti-Semitism in Germany and Austria.* New York: John Wiley, 1964.

Reichman, Eva. *Hostages of Civilization: The Social Sources of National Socialist Anti-Semitism.* Boston: Beacon, 1951.

V. Miscellaneous Topics: Monographs and Documents

Avotins, Evian, J. Dzirkalis and V. Petersons. *Daugavas Vanagi: Who Are They?* Riga: Latvian State Publishing House, 1963.

Bernadotte, Count Folke. *The Curtain Falls: Last Days of the Third Reich.* Translated from the Swedish. New York: Knopf, 1945.

Elkin, Michael. *Forged in Fury.* New York: Ballantine Books, 1971.

Feingold, Henry L. *The Politics of Rescue: The Roosevelt Administration and the Holocaust, 1938 - 1945.* New Brunswick, New Jersey: Rutgers University Press, 1970.

Friedlaender, Saul. *Pius XII and The Third Reich: A Documentation.* Translated from the French and German. New York: Knopf, 1966.

Friedman, Philip. "Jewish Resistance." *Yad Veshem Studies* II (1958), 113-131.

Halperin, Irving. *Messengers from the Dead.* Philadelphia: Westminster Press, 1970.

Hausner, Gideon. *Justice in Jerusalem.* New York: Schocken Books, 1968.

Katz, Robert. *Black Sabbath: A Journey through a Crime against Humanity.* New York: Macmillan, 1969.

Kusnetsov, Anatol. *Babi Yar.* Translated from the Russian. New York: Dial Press, 1967.

Levinson, Isaac. *The Untold Story.* Johannesburg: Kayor Publishing House, 1958.

Lewy, Guenther. *The Catholic Church and Nazi Germany.* New York: McGraw-Hill, 1964.

Maurina, Zenta. *Die Eisernen Riegel Zerbrechen.* Memmingen: Maximilian Dietrich Verlag, 1957.

Monneray, Henri, ed. *La persecution des Juifs dans les pays de l'Est.* Paris: Edition du Centre, 1949.

Monneray, Henri, ed. *La persecution des Juifs en France et dans les autres pays de l'Ouest.* Paris: Edition du Centre, 1947.

Morse, Arthur D. *While Six Millions Died: A Chronicle of American Apathy.* New York: Random House, 1967.

Moser, Jonny. *Die Judenverfolgung in Oesterreich, 1938 - 1945.* Vienna: Europa Verlag, 1966.

Ruhm von Oppen, Beate. "Nazis and Christians." *World Politics,* XXI, 3 (April 1969), 392-424.

Schwarz, Leo W. ed. *The Root and the Bough: The Epic of an Enduring People.* New York: Rinehart, 1949.

Silabriedis, J. and B. Arklans. *Political Refugees Unmasked.* Riga: Latvian State Publishing House, 1965.

The Jews in Latvia. Tel-Aviv: D. Ben-Nun Press, 1971.

Tenenbaum, Dr. Joseph. *Underground.* New York: Philosophical Library, 1952.

Zahn, Gordon C. *German Catholics and Hitler's Wars: A Study in Social Control.* New York, 1962.

VI. The Ghettos

Bloom, Solomon F. "Dictator of the Lodz Ghetto: The Strange History of Mordechai Chaim Rumkowski." *Commentary,* VII, 2 (February 1949), 111-222.

Deschner, Guenther. *Menschen im Ghetto.* Gueterslow, Germany: Bertelsmann Sachbuchverlag Reinhard Mohn, 1969.

Friedman, Philip. "Problems of Research in Jewish Self-Government 'Judenrat' in the Nazi Period." *Yad Veshem Studies,* II (1958), 95-113.

Gringanz, Samuel. "Some Methodological Problems in the Study of the Ghetto." *Jewish Social Studies,* XII, 1 (January 1950), 65-72.

Kaplan, J. "Arms in the Riga Ghetto." *Fun letztn hurbn* I, 4 (November 1946), 4-6.

Trunk, Isaish. *Judenrat.* New York: McMillan Co., 1972.

Wiesenthal, Simon. *The Murderers Among Us.* Edited by Joseph Wechsberg. New York: McGraw-Hill, 1967.

Wulf, Josef. *Lodz: Das Letzte Ghetto auf Polnischem Boden.* Schriftenreihe der Bundeszentrale fuer Heimatdienst, Heft 59. Bonn, 1962.

VII. Concentration Camps

Arendt, Hannah. "Social Science Techniques and the Study of

Concentration Camps." *Jewish Social Studies,* XII, 1 (January 1950), 49-64.

Bettelheim, Bruno. "Individual and Mass Behavior in Extreme Situations." *Journal of Abnormal and Social Psychology,* XXXVIII, 3 (March 1943), 417-452.

Cohen, Elie A. *Human Behavior in the Concentration Camp.* Translated from the Dutch. New York: Grosset and Dunlap, Universal Library, 1960.

Death Camp Salaspils. Riga: Publishing House Liesma, 1960.

Eitinger, Dr. Leo, Matussek, Dr. Paul, and Dr. Helmut Paul. "Das K.Z. Syndrom," *Der Spiegel,* nos. 10, 11, 12, 1958.

"Le systeme concentrationaire allemand, 1940 - 1944." *Revue d'Histoire de la Deuzieme Guerre Mondiale,* nos. 15 and 16, 1954.

Michel, Henri. "The Need for a History of the Nazi Concentration Camp System." *Yad Veshem Bulletin,* no. 17 (December 1965), 4-8.

Poliakov, Leon. "The Mind of the Mass Murderer." *Commentary,* XII, 5 (November 1951), 451-459.

Przewodnik po upamietnionych miejscach walk i meczenstwa: Lata wojny 1939 - 1945 [Guide to remember places, battles and suffering: War years 1939 - 1945]. Warsaw: Drukarnia Narodowa, 1966.

Schneider, Gertrude. "Memoirs and Diaries of the Holocaust." *Herzl Institute Bulletin,* X, 28 (April 1973), 2-7.

Schneider, Gertrude. "Survival and Guilt Feelings of Jewish Concentration Camp Victims." *Jewish Social Studies,* XXXVII, 1 (1975), 74-83.

Index